Grammar Girl's™

QUICK and DIRTY TIPS™

FOR BETTER WRITING

Grammar Girl's™

St. Martin's Griffin
New York

MIGNON FOGARTY

QUICK and DIRTY TIPS™ FOR BETTER WRITING

GRAMMAR GIRL'S QUICK AND DIRTY TIPS FOR BETTER WRITING. Copyright © 2008 by Mignon Fogarty, Inc.
All rights reserved. Printed in the United States of America. For information, address
St. Martin's Press, 175 Fifth Avenue, New York, N.Y. 10010.

www.stmartins.com

Grammar Girl, Money Girl, Modern Manners Guy, and Quick and Dirty Tips are trademarks of
Mignon Fogarty, Inc.

Designed by Linda Kosarin
Interior art by Arnie Ten

The Library of Congress has cataloged the Henry Holt edition as follows:

Fogarty, Mignon.
    Grammar Girl's quick and dirty tips for better writing / Mignon Fogarty.—1st Holt pbk. ed.
        p.   cm.
    Includes bibliographical references and index.
    ISBN 978-0-8050-8831-1
1. English language—Grammar.   2. English language—Rhetoric.   3. Report writing.
I. Title.   II. Title: Quick and dirty tips for better writing.
    PE1112.F613   2008
    808'.042—dc22

                                                                        2008000695

ISBN 978-0-8050-8831-1

9   10

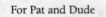
For Pat and Dude

Contents

Grammar Girl's™

QUICK and DIRTY TIPS™

FOR BETTER WRITING

Introduction

WE'RE ALL GOOD AT SOMETHING. My husband can calculate sales tax in his head, and surprisingly, it turns out I'm pretty good at teaching people about language. The revelation came to me slowly at first, and then in a tidal wave.

I had been working as an independent writer and editor for years when one day at the coffeehouse I decided it would be fun to call myself Grammar Girl and produce a short podcast with fun tips to help people remember simple language rules—the things I saw people mess up over and over again: *who* versus *whom, affect* versus *effect,* how to use semi-colons, and other mistakes of that sort. In its simplest form, a podcast is an audio program that is available on the Internet, and producing one seemed like a fun hobby for a girl who already had recording equipment from another project and already corrected errors for a living.

And then—Holy Internets, Batman—the audience at iTunes found me, figuratively threw me on their shoulders, and yelled "Hurray!" until the national media couldn't help but notice. Based entirely on word of mouth, the Grammar Girl podcast soon rose to #2 at iTunes, and with a little help from articles in *The Wall Street Journal* and CNN.com, it reached #1 and I signed a book deal.

The tidal wave didn't stop. I was sitting at my desk one day, minding my own business, when I got a call from a producer at the *Oprah Winfrey Show*. She wanted me to come to Chicago and be a guest on the show to answer language questions they had received from listeners. Things like that don't happen to girls like me! I said yes; and together my publisher and I cranked out a *Grammar Girl* audiobook to correspond with my appearance. It did well.

The stories continued, and the podcast was covered in *USA Today, BusinessWeek, The New York Times,* and many other outlets. Every time I was sure it would be the last. (How many people could there possibly be who were interested in grammar?) But so far they've kept coming.

All the while I have continued to put out a free show each week with a quick and dirty tip to help people write better, produce an e-mail newsletter with an additional tip, and oversee the entire Quick and Dirty Tips Network, which has grown out of the original Grammar Girl series. And of course, I've been writing this book.

I've spent a fair amount of time (too much time, really) pondering why so many people are excited about my little podcast. From what I can gather, the fun and friendly nature of the show plays an important role, and the need to write well is greater than it has been in a long time. We're writing more often than people did twenty years ago because e-mail and text messaging have taken the place of phone calls, and blogging is a popular pastime. We're all "professional" writers these days because our coworkers, friends, and family judge us on our writing, and we all secretly fear that we could do a better job.

This book is not intended to be a comprehensive style guide like *The Chicago Manual of Style* or *Garner's Modern American Usage* (both useful books for truly professional writers). This is a practical guide for everyday writers. I once gave everyone on my Christmas list batteries and film; I am nothing if not practical. So I'm giving you the batteries and film of language—the things everyone will use. I won't have my tips returned for cash or hidden on the closet shelf to be hauled out when I come over for dinner!

My philosophy is that learning about language should be fun. I'm not in this for the thrill of running a metaphorical red pen through e-mail messages or blog posts. Although writing badly is like dressing in lime skorts and an orange plaid sweater—people notice—publicly correcting a stranger's writing is as rude as asking someone with a fashion problem "Did you think that looked good when you got dressed this morning?" I would do neither. Instead, I hope to raise the waters of good writing by distributing quick and dirty tips as widely as possible. Really, I can't resist: I get flashes of crazy memory tricks, funny phrases, and cartoons where Aardvark (a blue aardvark) and Squiggly (a yellow snail) go on grammar adventures, and I love to share them all with you.

Chapter 1
DIRTY WORDS

EVEN THOUGH MY SHOW is called "Grammar Girl," the secret is that it's not usually grammar that confounds people—it's usage. I get complaints from purists, but *Usage Girl* doesn't have the same ring to it as *Grammar Girl,* and my books and podcasts aren't for purists anyway—they're for people who actually need help. Usage is about choosing the right word or phrase. It's something teachers generally expect you to pick up on your own, and it's the thing you're most likely to get skewered for if you screw up. (Life is so unfair!) I don't recall ever being taught the difference between *affect* and *effect,* for example; I was just expected to know.

Certain words are more difficult than others. I call them the dirty words, and we're going to tackle them here.

An Honorable Challenge: *A* Versus *An*

A lot of people learned the rule that you put *a* before words that start with consonants and *an* before words that start with vowels, but it's actually a bit more complicated than that.

The actual rule is that you use *a* before words that start with a consonant *sound* and *an* before words that start with a vowel *sound*.

> **Squiggly waited for *an* hour.**
>
> **Aardvark was on *a* historic expedition.**

An hour is correct because *hour* starts with a vowel sound. People seem to most commonly get tripped up by words that start with the letters *h* and *u* because sometimes these words start with vowel sounds and sometimes they start with consonant sounds. For example, it is *a historic expedition* because *historic* starts with an *h* sound, but it is *an honorable fellow* because *honorable* starts with an *o* sound.

> **Squiggly had *a* Utopian idea.**
>
> **Aardvark reminded him it's *an* unfair world.**

The letters *o* and *m* can be tricky too. Usually you put *an* before words that start with *o*, but sometimes you use *a*. For example, you would use *a* if you were to say, "She has a one-track mind," because *one-track* starts with a *w* sound.

> **Squiggly wants to work as *a* missionary.**
>
> **Aardvark wants to get *an* MBA.**

Other letters can also be pronounced either way. Just remember it is the *sound* that governs whether you use *a* or *an*, not the first letter of the word.

Pronunciation Wars

Since pronunciation is what guides the choice between *a* and *an*, people in different regions, where pronunciations are different, can come to different conclusions about which is the appropriate word.

Many pronunciation differences exist between British and American English. For example, the word for a certain kind of plant is pronounced "erb" in American English and "her-b" in British English.

Even within the United States there can be regional pronunciation differences. Although the majority of people pronounce the *h* in *historic*, some people on the East Coast pronounce *historic* as "istoric" and thus argue that *an historic monument* is the correct form.

In the rare cases where this is a problem, use the form that will be expected in your country or by the majority of your readers.

Definitely!

A and *an* are called indefinite articles. *The* is called a definite article. The difference is that *a* and *an* don't say anything special about the word that follows. For example, think about the sentence "I need *a* horse." You'll take any horse—just a horse will do. But if you say, "I need *the* horse," then you want a specific horse. That's why *the* is called a definite article—you want something definite. At least that's how I remember the name.

Tweedle Thee and Tweedle Thuh

I find it interesting that there are two indefinite articles to choose from (*a* and *an*) depending on the word that comes next, but there is only one definite article (*the*). But there's a special pronunciation rule about *the* that is similar to the rule about when to use *a* and *an*: *The* is pronounced "thuh" when it comes before a word that starts with a consonant sound, and it's pronounced "thee" when it comes before a word that starts with a vowel sound. It can also be pronounced "thee" for emphasis, for example, if you wanted to say, "Twitter is the [pronounced "thee"] hot social networking tool." I actually have trouble remembering this rule and have to make special marks in my podcast scripts to remind myself to get the pronunciation right. I think I must have missed the day they covered this in school, and I've never recovered.

A LOT OF TROUBLE: *ALOT* VERSUS *A LOT* VERSUS *ALLOT*

The correct spelling is "a lot."

> *Alot* **is not a word.**
>
> *A lot* **means "a large number."**
>
> *Allot* **means "to parcel out."**

I WOULD NEVER AFFECT INTEREST JUST FOR EFFECT: *AFFECT* VERSUS *EFFECT*

If you don't know the difference between *affect* and *effect,* don't worry—you're not alone. These two words are consistently among the most searched for words in online dictionaries, and I get at least one e-mail message a week asking me to explain the difference. In fact, the confusion over *affect* and *effect* could be why *impact* has emerged to mean "affect" in business writing: people give up trying to figure out the difference between *affect* and *effect* and rewrite their sentences, unfortunately substituting an equally inappropriate word. (See "Impact," page 33.)

The difference between *affect* and *effect* is actually pretty straightforward: the majority of the time you use *affect* as a verb and *effect* as a noun.

Affect most commonly means something like "to influence" or "to change."

The arrows affected Aardvark.

The rain affected Squiggly's plans.

Affect can also mean, roughly, "to act in a way that you don't feel," as in *He affected an air of superiority*.

Effect has a lot of subtle meanings as a noun, but to me the meaning "a result" seems to be at the core of most of the definitions.

The effect was eye-popping.

The sound effects were amazing.

The rain had no effect on Squiggly's plans.

So most of the time *affect* is a verb and *effect* is a noun. There are rare instances where the roles are switched, but this is "Quick and Dirty"

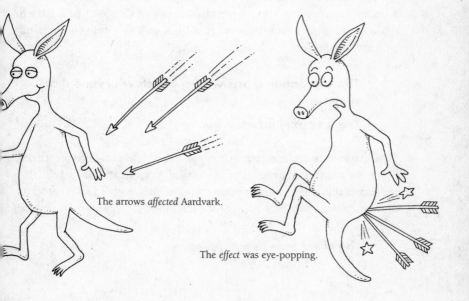

The arrows *affected* Aardvark.

The *effect* was eye-popping.

grammar, not comprehensive grammar, and if you stick with the verb-noun rule, you'll be right about 95 percent of the time.

An Effective Memory Trick

For our purposes, *affect* is a verb and *effect* is a noun. Now we can get to the memory tricks. First, get this image in your mind: the raven flew down the avenue. Why? Because the letters *a-v-e-n* (in both *raven* and *avenue*) are the same first letters as "affect verb effect noun"!

Need another one? Because *effect* is usually a noun, that means you can usually put an article in front of it and the sentence will still make sense. Look at these examples:

The effect is eye-popping.

He kissed her for [the] effect.

In both of these cases *effect* is a noun and you can put *the* in front of it without making the sentence completely weird. *The* isn't necessary in the second example, but it doesn't ruin the sentence. On the other hand, look at these sentences where *affect* is a verb:

The eye-popping arrow [the] affects everyone that way.

The kiss [the] affected her.

You can't insert the direct article, *the,* before *affect* in those sentences, which means you want to use the verb (*affect*), not the noun (*effect*). I remember this rule by remembering that *the* ends with *e* and *effect* starts with *e*, so the two *e*'s butt up against each other.

The effect was eye-popping.

Exception Alert

Affect can be used as a noun when you are talking about psychology. It means the mood that someone appears to have. For example, a doctor may say, "The patient displayed a happy *affect*." Psychologists find the word useful because they can never really know what someone else is feeling. Technically, they can only know how someone appears to be feeling.

Effect can be used as a verb that essentially means "to bring about," or "to accomplish." For example, you could say, "Aardvark hoped to *effect* change within the burrow."

ALTHOUGH IT'S NOT A REAL RULE, IT STILL BOTHERS ME: *ALTHOUGH* VERSUS *WHILE*

I often have to tell people their pet peeves aren't actually hard-and-fast grammar rules. I have to tell people it's OK to split infinitives, and in some cases it's fine to end a sentence with a preposition.

I know it's upsetting to find out your nearest and dearest beliefs are wrong because I have my own mistaken pet peeve: it bugs me no end when people use *while* to mean *although,* but however hard I looked, I couldn't convince myself I was right. The horror!

You see, I believe *although* means "in spite of the fact that," as in *Although the tree was tall, Squiggly and Aardvark thought they could make it to the top. Although* is what's called a concessive conjunction, meaning that it is used to express a concession. On the other hand, I believe that *while* should be reserved to mean "at the same time," as in *While Squiggly gathered wood, Aardvark hid the maracas.*

At first I was sure I was right because Eric Partridge said in his book *Usage and Abusage* that "*while* for *although* is a perverted use of the correct sense of *while,* which properly means 'at the same time.'"

Ha!

But then I discovered that *Fowler's Modern English Usage* states it is normal and acceptable to use *while* to mean "although." Fowler even called Partridge's comment "indefensible." It's a grammar rumble, people.

I decided to go over their heads and see what the *Oxford English Dictionary* has to say, and it backs up *Fowler* with an entry stating that *while* can mean "although." Two additional dictionaries concurred. I was thwarted, but I'd given it a good shot.

One reason I'm telling you this story is that I want you to know that I go to this much trouble to validate all of your pet peeves too, but sometimes it isn't possible.

My only small vindication is that there are sentences where it is confusing to use *while* to mean "although," and then it isn't allowed. For example, if you said, "While Squiggly is yellow, Aardvark is blue," people wouldn't know whether you were contrasting their colors or saying that Aardvark is only blue *when* Squiggly is yellow. In cases like that, you have to use *although*.

So, moving forward, I will continue to reserve *while* for times when I mean "at the same time"—old habits are hard to break—but I will now refrain from striking out *while* every chance I get. I wonder if the Modern Manners Guy will want me to send apology cards to all the writers I terrorized about this over the years. I hope not!

Next, I have two related bonus facts for you.

First, there isn't any difference between *although* and *though* when they are being used as described above. *Though* is a less formal version of *although*, but it's in such common use that it's OK to use it in formal writing too.

Second, *while* and *whilst* both mean the same thing. Although *whilst* is still used in British English, it is considered archaic in American English. It's just a language quirk that *whilst* survived in Britain but perished in America.

I ASSURE YOU I WILL ENSURE EVERYONE HAS INSURANCE: *ASSURE* VERSUS *ENSURE* VERSUS *INSURE*

Assure, ensure, and *insure* have the same underlying meaning, but they each have a slightly different use.

Assure is the only one of the three words that means "to reassure someone or to promise."

I assure you that the chocolate is fresh.

Ensure chiefly means "to make certain or to guarantee."

He must ensure that the effect is eye-popping.

Insure can be interchangeable with ensure in some cases, but it is easiest to keep these words straight by reserving insure for references to insurance.

I need to insure my car.

The definitions are different in British English: in Britain, *assure* can mean "to *insure* against a loss."

ABANDON YOUR BACKWARD WAYS: *BACKWARD* VERSUS *BACKWARDS*

When *backward* and *backwards* are used to describe verbs, both words are correct and interchangeable.

The children moved backward/backwards.

Count backward/backwards from ten to one.

The *s* is more common in Britain than in the United States, so you should consider what the convention is in your country and use *backwards* in Britain and *backward* in the United States. This regional difference is one reason you're probably confused. If you read *The New York Times* and *BBC* websites in the same day, you could see the word used both ways.

The exception is that you never use the *s* when you use *backward* as an adjective (in other words, to describe a noun). It is always *backward* as an adjective.

They couldn't understand the peeves' backward ways.

Aardvark wondered if the program had backward compatibility.

So if you are in the United States, you have it easier because you can just remember that it's always *backward,* without the *s*, not *backwards.* We like shortcuts here, like drive-through restaurants, so you can remember that we've lopped off the *s*. But, if you are using British English, then you have to remember that it's *backwards* as an adverb and *backward* as an adjective.

The story is similar for the words *toward* and *towards:* both are correct and interchangeable, and you can use either one because they mean the same thing. The *s* is more common in Britain than in the United States, so you should take into account what the convention is in your country and use *towards* in Britain and *toward* in the United States. Again, a memory trick can be to remember that Americans like shortcuts.

I FEEL BAD: *BAD* VERSUS *BADLY*

Interviewers often ask if people are afraid to write to me, and the answer, sadly, is yes. I get a lot of e-mail messages in which people (even my mother!) include blanket requests for forgiveness for any unidentified grammar errors. I feel bad about that—my goal isn't to make people self-conscious or afraid.

In addition, I get skewered when I make an error (or perceived error) myself. So when I was quoted in an article saying, "I feel bad about that," a lot of readers saw a chance to send me a gotcha e-mail message about using *bad* to modify *feel*. They maintained that I should have said, "I feel *badly* about that." I'm not perfect, and I make lots of errors (especially in live interviews), but this isn't one of them.

The quick and dirty tip is that it is correct to say you feel bad when you are expressing an emotion. To say "I feel badly" could imply that there's something wrong with your sense of touch. Every time I hear people say, "I feel badly," I imagine them in a dark room having trouble feeling their way around with numb fingers.

I get that image because *badly* is an adverb, meaning that it modifies a verb (adverbs sometimes modify adjectives and other adverbs too). So when you say, "I feel badly," the adverb *badly* relates to the action verb *feel*. Since the action verb *feel* can mean "to touch things," feeling *badly* can mean you're having trouble touching things.

This is a problem with most of the verbs that describe senses such as taste and smell. Consider the different meanings of these two sentences:

I smell bad.

I smell badly.

When you say, "I smell badly," *badly* is an adverb that modifies the verb *smell*. You're saying your sniffer isn't working, just as when you say you feel badly you're saying your fingers aren't working. When you say, "I smell bad," *bad* is an adjective, which means it modifies a noun. You're saying you stink, just as when you say, "I feel bad," you're saying you are regretful or sad or ill or wicked.

The reason people often think they should say they feel badly is that it's only after linking verbs such as *feel, smell,* and *am* that you use an adjective such as *bad*. With most other verbs, it's correct to use the adverb. For example, if you gave a horrible speech, you could say, "It went badly." If a child threw a fit in a shopping mall, it would be correct to say, "She behaved badly." The quick and dirty tip is to remember the following:

Adjectives follow linking verbs.

Adverbs modify action verbs.

See pages 31 and 144 for further discussion about linking verbs.

CHOOSE BETWEEN THE BEES AND THE TWEENS: *BETWEEN* VERSUS *AMONG*

There is a difference between *between* and *among:* you use *between* when you are writing about two things and *among* when you are writing about more than two things. That's a quick and dirty tip, and there are exceptions, but if you remember that *between* is for two things and *among* is for more than two things, then you'll be right most of the time.

I'm expecting to hear a collective groan about the corny mnemonic that I'm going to give you, but I do think it will help you remember when to use the word *between.* Here's the sentence: *Squiggly dreaded choosing between the bees and the tweens.* The idea is that Squiggly is choosing between two different groups—bees and tweens—and the correct word is *between.*

Here's a bonus: the difference between *among* and *amongst* is similar to the difference between *while* and *whilst. Amongst* is more common in British English and is considered old-fashioned or archaic in American English.

The Inbetweeners

For those of you who may not know, *tween* is a word that's used to describe kids who are at that weird stage between childhood and their teenage years. Depending on whom you ask, a tween can be a youth who is anywhere from eight to fourteen years old.

I know some of you will be wondering about the exception to that rule. Here's the deal: you can use the word *between* when you are talking about distinct, individual items even if there are more than two of them. For example, you would say, "She chose *between* Harvard, Brown, and Yale," because the colleges are individual items she is choosing between. On the other hand, if you were talking about the colleges collectively you would say, "She chose *among* the Ivy League schools."

BRING IT ON: *BRING VERSUS TAKE*

I received a comment about *bring* versus *take* that I found especially interesting from a man named Farrel, who is from an unspecified country. His impression is that everyone in his home country knows the difference between *bring* and *take,* and it's just Americans who don't seem to be able to get it right. I don't know if that's true, but I'll take his word for it and try to do my part to fix the problem.

Whether you use *bring* or *take* depends on your point of reference for the action. The quick and dirty tip is that you ask people to bring things to the place you are, and you take things to the place you are going. For example, I would ask Aardvark to bring Squiggly to my party next week, and then Aardvark would call Squiggly and ask, "May I take you to Grammar Girl's party?"

I am asking Aardvark to bring Squiggly because I am at the destination—from my perspective, Aardvark is bringing someone here. Aardvark is offering to take Squiggly because he is transporting Squiggly to a remote destination—from Aardvark's perspective, he is taking someone there.

Here are two examples that help me remember.

First, think of a restaurant where you order food to go. It's often informally called getting "takeout." When you get take-out food, you're moving the food from your location (the restaurant) to somewhere else (a destination). And it's take-out food, not bring-out food. You're taking the food to a destination.

Second, if I'm sitting at home feeling lazy, wishing dinner would appear, I would say, "I wish someone would bring me dinner." I imagine Pat stopping at a restaurant and getting dinner to go. From my perspective, he is bringing me dinner because dinner is coming to my location.

I suspect that one reason people get confused about *bring* and *take* is that there are many exceptions to the basic rules. For example, idioms such as *bring home the bacon* and *take a bath* and phrasal verbs such as *bring up, bring about, take down,* and *take after* don't comply with the rule that *bring* means to cause something to go to the speaker and *take* means to cause something to go away from the speaker.

Nevertheless, when your point is that something is being moved from one location to another, the rule is that things are brought to the speaker and taken away from the speaker. You ask people to bring things to you, and you take things to other people. You ask people to bring you coffee, and you offer to take the dishes to the kitchen. You tell people to bring you good news, and you take your camera to the beach.

As an aside, the past tense of *bring* is *brought,* as in *He brought me dinner.* In some regions people say *brung* or *brang,* but those words aren't standard English.

Finally, an interesting note is that the words *come* and *go* follow rules that are similar to those for *bring* and *take. Come* is like *bring:* you ask people to come here—to come to where you are. And *go* is like *take:* you tell people to go away—to move away from your location. Aardvark and Squiggly will come to my party, and when Aardvark calls Squiggly, he'll say, "Let's go to Grammar Girl's party."

If You Must Use Bad Grammar, Don't Do It By Accident: *By Accident* Versus *On Accident*

Some of the most difficult questions I get are from people who didn't grow up speaking English and who want to know why we use a particular preposition in a specific phrase. Why do we say *I'm in bed* instead of *I'm on bed*? Do people suffer *from a disease* or suffer *with a disease*? Are we *in a restaurant* or *at a restaurant?* I'm a native English speaker, so my first thought is usually something like, "I don't know why; *in bed* just sounds right," and sometimes either option seems correct.

But there's one question I am able to answer—Why do some people say "on accident" and some people say "by accident"?—because I was lucky enough to find an entire research paper on the topic, published by Leslie Barratt, a professor of linguistics at Indiana State University.*

According to Barratt's study, use of the two different versions appears to be distributed by age. Whereas *on accident* is common in people under thirty-five, almost no one over forty says *on accident.* Most older people say *by accident.* It's quite amazing: the study says that *on* is more prevalent under age ten, both *on* and *by* are common between the ages of ten and thirty-five, and *by* is overwhelmingly preferred by those over thirty-five. (I'm over thirty-five, and I definitely prefer *by accident.*)

An interesting conclusion from the paper is that although there are some hypotheses, nobody really knows why younger people all over the United States started saying *on accident* instead of *by accident.* For example, there's the idea that *on accident* is parallel to *on purpose,* but nobody has proven that children all across the country started speaking differently from their parents because they were seeking parallelism. Although I have no proof, I suspect that it must have something to do with nationwide media since it is such a widespread age-related phenomenon. *Barney & Friends* hasn't been on TV long enough to be the culprit, and *Sesame Street* has been on TV too long to be the culprit. Really, all we can say is that it's just one of those language things that happens sometimes.

Although *on accident* grates on the ears of many adults, Barratt found that there is no widespread stigma associated with saying *on accident.* So it seems to me that as the kids who say *on accident* grow up

---

* L. Barratt, "What Speakers Don't Notice: Language Changes Can Sneak In," in *Innovation and Continuity in Language and Communication of Different Language Cultures,* ed. Rudolf Muhr (New York: Peter Lang, 2006). Also in TRANS 16/2005: http://www.inst.at/trans/16Nr/01_4/barratt16.htm (accessed June 13, 2007).

(some of whom are even unaware that *by accident* is an option, let alone the preferred phrase of grown-ups), *on accident* will become the main, accepted phrase. By that time, there won't be enough of us left who say *by accident* to correct them!

THE CAN-CAN DANCE: *CAN* VERSUS *MAY*

Legions of exasperated teachers have responded, "May I go to the bathroom!" when children raise their hands and ask, "Can I go to the bathroom?" Technically, *can* is used to ask if something is possible, and *may* is used to ask if something is permissible. So yes, those kids *can* go to the bathroom (we hope!); what they need is to know if they have their teachers' permission to proceed—if they *may* go to the bathroom. Nevertheless, substituting *can* for *may* is done so commonly it can hardly be considered wrong. This is what I call a cover letter grammar topic—use *may* when you are in formal situations or want to be especially proper, but don't get too hung up about it in everyday life.

A CAPITOL IDEA: *CAPITAL* VERSUS *CAPITOL*

When the noun *capitol* ends with an *-ol*, it is referring to state capitol *buildings* or the Capitol building in Washington, D.C. You can remember that the rotunda of the Capitol *building* is round like the letter *o*.

The other kind of *capital,* with an *-al* at the end, refers to uppercase letters, wealth, or a city that is the seat of government for its region or is important in some way. Don't get confused by the fact that *capital* with an *-al* is used for a capital city and *capitol* with an *-ol* is used for a state's capitol building. Just remember that *capitol* with an *-ol* refers only to buildings, and fix in your mind that image of the round, *o*-like rotunda of the U.S. Capitol building. (See page 138 for rules about capitalizing *capitol*.)

I LIKE TO GIVE COMPLIMENTS:
COMPLIMENT VERSUS COMPLEMENT

Imagine the voice of a movie trailer announcer: "Two words. One pronunciation. In a world where choosing the right word can mean life or death, Squiggly must make a decision: *i* or *e*."

OK. You can stop imagining the corny voice now. Fortunately for Squiggly, I have a great memory trick for remembering the difference between *compliment* and *complement*. A compliment (with an *i*) is a word of praise, so just remember the sentence

I like to give compliments.

Complement (with an *e*) means that something pairs well with something else. You can remember the meaning by thinking things that complement each other often complete each other, and *complement* and *complete* both have *e*'s in them.

Things that complement each other often complete each other.

IT'S DECEPTIVELY INFLAMMABLE:
WORDS THAT SHOULD BE BANNED

If you write that a crossword puzzle is deceptively easy, does that mean it is easy or hard? The answer is that using the word *deceptively* can lead to confusion, and the best approach is to rewrite the sentence.

There's a similar story for the word *inflammable*. Some people think it means "easy to burn" and other people think it means "resistant to burning." It's best to avoid it altogether.

PEOPLE FEAR THINGS THAT ARE DIFFERENT: *DIFFERENT FROM* VERSUS *DIFFERENT THAN*

Different from is preferred to *different than*. I remember this by remembering that *different* has two *f*'s and only one *t*, so the best choice between *than* and *from* is the one that starts with an *f*.

Squiggly knew he was di_ff_erent _f_rom the other snails.

IN OTHER WORDS, GET IT RIGHT: *I.E.* VERSUS *E.G.*

Misusing *i.e.* and *e.g.* is one of the top five mistakes I used to see when editing technical documents. People are so mixed up (and so certain in their confusion) that I would get back drafts from clients where they had actually crossed out the right abbreviation and replaced it with the wrong one. I had to just laugh.

I.e. and *e.g.* are both abbreviations for Latin terms. *I.e.* stands for *id est* and means "that is." *E.g.* stands for *exempli gratia*, which means roughly "for example." "Great. Latin," you're probably thinking. "How am I supposed to remember that?"

But by now, I'm sure you know that I'm not going to ask you to remember Latin. I'm going to give you a memory trick! So here's how I remember the difference. Forget about *i.e.* standing for "that is." From now on, to you, *i.e.*, which starts with *i*, means "in other words," and *e.g.*, which starts with *e*, means "for example."

Starts with _i_ = _in_ other words

Starts with _e_ = _e_xample

A few listeners have also written in to say they remember the difference between *i.e.* and *e.g.* by imagining that *i.e.* means "in essence," and noting that *e.g.* sounds like "egg," as in "egg-sample," and those are good memory tricks too.

So now that you have a few tricks for remembering what the abbreviations mean, let's think about how to use them in a sentence.

E.g. means "for example," so you use it to introduce an example:

Aardvark likes card games, e.g., bridge and crazy eights.

Squiggly visited Ivy League colleges, e.g., Harvard and Yale.

Because I used *e.g.*, you know I have provided a list of examples of card games that Aardvark likes and colleges Squiggly visited. It's not a definitive list of all card games Aardvark likes or colleges Squiggly visited; it's just a few examples.

On the other hand, *i.e.* means "in other words," so you use it to introduce a further clarification:

Aardvark likes to play cards, i.e., bridge and crazy eights.

Squiggly visited Ivy League colleges, i.e., Harvard and Yale.

Because I used *i.e.*, which introduces a clarification, you know that these are the only two card games Aardvark enjoys and the only two colleges Squiggly visited.

Here are two more examples:

Squiggly loves watching old cartoons (e.g., DuckTales and Tugboat Mickey). The words following *e.g.* are examples, so you know that they are just some of the old cartoons Squiggly enjoys.

Squiggly loves watching Donald Duck's nephews (i.e., Huey, Dewey, and Louie). The words following *i.e.* provide clarification: they tell you the names of Donald Duck's three nephews.

An important point is that if I've failed, and you're still confused about when to use each abbreviation, you can always just write out the words "for example" or "in other words." There's no rule that says you have to use the abbreviations.

Here are a few other things about *i.e.* and *e.g.* Don't italicize them; even though they are abbreviations for Latin words, they've been used for so long that they're considered a standard part of the English language. (*I.e.* and *e.g.* are italicized in this section because I use italics to highlight words that are being discussed as words instead of being used for their meaning.) Also, remember that they are abbreviations, and there is always a period after each letter.

Also, I always put a comma after *i.e.* and *e.g.* I've noticed that my spell checker always freaks out and wants me to remove the comma, but five out of six style guides recommend using the comma.

Finally, I tend to reserve *i.e.* and *e.g.* to introduce parenthetical statements, but it's also perfectly fine to use *i.e.* and *e.g.* in other ways. You can put a comma before them, or if you use them to introduce a main clause that follows another main clause, you can put a semicolon before them. You can even put an em dash before *i.e.* and *e.g.* if you are using them to introduce something dramatic. They're just abbreviations for words, so you can use them in any way you'd use the words *in essence* or *for example*.

I WANT EACH OF YOU TO WIN: *EACH* VERSUS *EVERY*

Each and *every* mean the same thing and are considered singular nouns, so they take singular verbs. (Note the singular verbs in the following examples.) If you want to get technical, you can use *each* to emphasize the individual items or people:

Each car is handled with care.

and *every* to emphasize the larger group:

Every car should use hybrid technology.

People often say "each and every" for emphasis, but it is redundant.

EVERYONE LOVES SQUIGGLY: *EVERYONE* VERSUS *EVERYBODY*

Everyone and *everybody* mean the same thing: every person. You can use them interchangeably and they are considered singular.

Everyone loves Squiggly.

Everybody is coming over after the parade.

FARTHER THAN YOU'VE EVER GONE BEFORE: *FURTHER* VERSUS *FARTHER*

The quick and dirty tip here is that you use *farther* to talk about physical distance and *further* to talk about metaphorical or figurative distance. It's easy to remember because *farther* has the word *far* in it, and *far* obviously relates to physical distance.

For example, you might say, "Squiggly and Aardvark walked to a town far, far away. After many miles, Squiggly grew tired. 'How much farther?' he asked in despair."

Did you see that? Squiggly used *farther* because he was asking about physical distance.

If Aardvark were frustrated with Squiggly, he might say, "Squiggly, I'm tired of your complaining; further, I'm tired of carrying your maracas." In this case, Aardvark used *further* because he isn't talking about physical distance, he's talking about metaphorical distance: further along the list of irritations.

Sometimes the quick and dirty tip breaks down because it's hard to decide whether you're talking about physical distance or not. For example, take a look at this sentence: *I'm further along in my book than you are in yours.* You could think of it as a physical distance through the pages and use *farther* or as a figurative distance through the story and use *further.*

The good news is that in these ambiguous cases it doesn't matter which word you choose. It's fine to use *further* and *farther* interchangeably when the distinction isn't clear. People have been using them interchangeably for hundreds of years!

Just remember that *farther* has a tie to physical distance and can't be used to mean "moreover" or "in addition." When I mean "in addition," I always use *furthermore* instead of *further.* Because *furthermore* and *farther* are more different from each other than *further* and *farther,* I never get confused.

> **Aardvark's feet hurt. *Furthermore,* Squiggly's complaining was driving him batty.**
>
> **He reminded Squiggly they didn't have much *farther* to go.**

An interesting side note is that in Britain people use the word *farther* much less than people do in the United States. At least one source speculates that this is because with British pronunciation, *farther* sounds too much like *father.*

I Am Woman, Hear Me Roar: *Female* Versus *Woman*

Regardless of your political beliefs, I believe everyone can agree that this has been an amazing year for women in politics. First, Nancy Pelosi became the first female Speaker of the House, and then Hillary Clinton became the first woman to have a good chance of becoming president of the United States.

Because of these events, writers have spilled a lot of ink on stories about female advances, which means I have received a lot of messages asking about correct use of *female* and *woman.*

Before I answer the usage question, I want to address a related issue, which is that some people may argue that it's sexist to point out these women's sex. They say that such language implies that it's unexpected that the Speaker would be a woman, in the way that saying someone is a male nurse or a female doctor wrongly implies that men aren't usually nurses or that women aren't usually doctors. But, given that Nancy Pelosi is, for example, actually the first woman to ever be Speaker of the House, I don't believe it's sexist to point out that she is a woman because that fact is an exciting and unique part of the story.

So then, what is the best way to talk about Nancy Pelosi being a woman? The word *woman* is primarily a noun, but it is also less commonly used as an adjective (which means in some cases it can be used to modify nouns).

A quick and dirty tip for testing the validity of using *woman* as an adjective in a particular sentence is to substitute the word *man* to see if it makes sense. For example, it sounds ridiculous to say someone is "the first man Speaker of the House." Of course, you would say "male Speaker of the House." So, even though it's not strictly wrong to use *woman* as an adjective, it's better to use the primary adjective, *female,* and say that Nancy Pelosi is the first female Speaker of the House.

IF THERE WERE FEWER GRAMMARIANS . . . : LESS VERSUS FEWER

Less and *fewer* are easy to mix up. They mean the same thing—the opposite of *more*—but you use them in different circumstances. The quick and dirty tip is that you use *less* with mass nouns and *fewer* with count nouns.

Count Nouns Versus Mass Nouns

I'm worried that I've scared you off, but it's easy to remember the difference between mass nouns and count nouns.

A count noun is just something you can count. I'm looking at my desk and I see books, pens, and M&M's. I can count all those things, so they are count nouns and the right word to use is *fewer*. I should eat fewer M&M's.

Mass nouns are just things that you can't count individually. Again, on my desk I see tape and clutter. Those things can't be counted individually, so the right word to use is *less*. If I had less clutter, my desk would be cleaner. Another clue is that you don't make mass nouns plural: I would never say I have clutters on my desk or that I need more tapes to hold my book covers together.

Sometimes it isn't obvious if something is a mass noun or a count noun because some words can be used in different ways. For example, *coffee* can refer to either a mass of liquid or a cup of liquid. If you're responsible for filling the coffee decanter at a wedding, and you're getting carried away, your boss may ask you to make less coffee. But if you're a waiter serving cups of coffee to the tables, and the crowd is waning, your boss may tell you to take out fewer coffees next time. She means cups of coffee, but it's common to hear that shortened to just coffee as in *Bring me a coffee, please*. Remember that I said mass nouns (such as *coffee*) can't be made plural? In this example, I've made a mass noun plural (*coffees*), but in the process I transformed it into a count noun. So the rule still holds.

Furniture is another tricky word; it isn't immediately obvious whether it is a mass noun or a count noun. If I think of a furniture store, I think of lots of individual pieces of furniture, but furniture is a collective name for a mass of stuff. You could say, "Look at all those chairs," but you would never say, "Look at all those furnitures." *Furniture* is a mass noun, and *chair* is a count noun. Therefore, you'd say, "We need less furniture in this dance hall. Can we have fewer chairs?"

Exceptions

There are exceptions to these rules; for example, even though we count hours, dollars, and miles, it is customary to use the word *less* to describe time, money, and distance (perhaps because these things can be divided into infinitely small units). For example, you could say, "That wedding reception lasted less than two hours. I hope they paid the band less than four hundred dollars." So keep in mind that time, money, and distance are different, but if you stick with the quick and dirty tip that *less* is for mass nouns and *fewer* is for count nouns, you'll be right most of the time.

Memory Tricks

There are two ways I remember when to use *less* and when to use *fewer*.

First, I think of the classic example of the grocery store express lane. Most of the signs for these lanes read, "10 items or less," and that's just wrong. The signs should read, "10 items or fewer," because items are individual, countable things. Between hearing people complain about the

There is *less* water in the lake. We'll have *fewer* fish for dinner.

signs and seeing the signs every week or so, it sticks in my head that it should be fewer items. And when I stand in line and count the fifteen items that belong to the person in front of me in the ten-items-or-fewer lane, I'm strongly reinforcing the idea that items are countable.

Second, I have a memory trick, and I've even had a cartoon drawn up so that you can see into my imagination. I think of Aardvark sitting by a lake. He's fishing. The water is low in the lake this year, so there is less water in the lake. You can't count water in a lake. *Less* and *lake* both begin with the letter *l*. There is less water in the lake. Squiggly is worried about dinner. Aardvark usually catches four fish, but what if there are only three? "We'll have fewer fish for dinner," Squiggly thinks to himself fretfully. You can count fish. *Fewer* and *fish* both start with the letter *f*, and Squiggly is counting fish in his head. They'll have fewer fish for dinner.

HOW YOU DOIN'?: *GOOD* VERSUS *WELL*

It's such a simple little question: *how are you?* But I've heard from people who feel a twinge of trepidation or even full-blown frustration every time they have to decide whether to say they're good or they're well.

"I'm good," is what you're likely to hear in general conversation, but there are grammar nitpickers out there who will chide you if you say it. The wonderful news is that those nitpickers are wrong: it's perfectly acceptable to say, "I'm good," and you shouldn't have to shamefully submit to teasing remarks such as the time-honored and leering, "How good are you?"

The nitpickers will tell you that *well* is an adverb (and therefore modifies verbs) and that *good* is an adjective (and therefore modifies nouns), but the situation isn't that simple.

The key is to understand how linking verbs differ from action verbs. (Trust me, this is worth it so you can look people in the eye and say, "I'm good," with absolute confidence.)

First, let's talk about action verbs. They're easy; they describe actions. Verbs such as *run, jump,* and *swim* are all action verbs. If you want to describe an action verb, you use an adverb such as *well*. You could say, "He runs well; she jumps well; they swim well." *Well* is an adverb that relates to all of those action verbs.

Linking verbs, on the other hand, are a bit more complicated. Linking verbs aren't about actions as much as they are about connecting other words together. They're also sometimes called "copulative verbs."

I think of the verb *to be* as the quintessential linking verb. The word *is* is a form of the verb *to be*, and if I say, "Squiggly is yellow," the main purpose of *is* is really just to link the word *Squiggly* with the word *yellow*. Other linking verbs include *seem, appear, look, become,* and verbs that describe senses, such as *feel* and *smell*. That isn't a comprehensive list of linking verbs—there are at least sixty in the English language—but I hope I've given you an idea of how they work. (See the appendix on page 198 for a list of common linking verbs.)

One complication is that some verbs—such as the sensing verbs—can be both linking verbs and action verbs. A trick that will help you figure out if you're dealing with a linking verb is to see if you can replace the verb with a form of *to be*; if so, then it's probably a linking verb.

For example, you can deduce that *feels* is a linking verb in the sentence *He feels bad* because if you replace *feels* with the word *is*, the sentence still makes sense:

He feels bad.

He is bad.

(The sentence makes sense; feels was a linking verb)

On the other hand, you can deduce that *feels* is an action verb in the sentence *He feels badly* because if you replace *feels* with *is*, the sentence doesn't make sense anymore:

He feels badly.

He is badly.

(The sentence doesn't make sense; feels was an action verb)

OK, so now you understand the difference between linking verbs and action verbs. That may seem like a detour on the way to learning why it is OK to say, "I'm good," but it's important because the thing people seem to forget is that it's standard to use adjectives—such as *good*—after linking verbs. When you do it, they are called predicate adjectives, and they refer back to the noun before the linking verb. That's why, even though *good* is primarily an adjective, it is OK to say, "I am good": *am* is a linking verb, and you use adjectives after linking verbs.

Aside from the linking-verb-action-verb trickiness, another reason people get confused about this topic is that *well* can be both an adverb and a predicate adjective. As I said earlier, in the sentence *He swam well, well* is an adverb that describes how he swam. But when you say, "I am well," you're using *well* as a predicate adjective. That's fine, but most sources say *well* is reserved to mean "healthy" when it's used in this way. So if you are recovering from a long illness and someone is inquiring about your health, it's appropriate to say, "I am well," but if you're just describing yourself on a generally good day and nobody's asking specifically about your health, a more appropriate response is, "I am good."

Finally, it's very important to remember that it's wrong to use *good* as an adverb after an action verb. For example, it's wrong to say, "He swam good." Cringe! The proper sentence is *He swam well,* because *swam* is an action verb and it needs an adverb to describe it. Remember, you can only use adjectives such as *good* and *bad* after linking verbs; you can't use them after action verbs.

LET'S GET THOSE KIDS GRADUATED: *GRADUATED* VERSUS *GRADUATED FROM*

Every graduation season I get e-mail messages complaining about people who say "Johnny graduated high school." And those complainers are right to be annoyed.

Although the *graduated high school* construction is becoming more common, it is incorrect. Here are the proper ways to use the verb *graduated:*

A school does the act of graduating a student: Stanford graduated thousands of students this year.

Students are graduated from a school: Squiggly graduated from Stanford.

If you want to be persnickety, you can also say a student was graduated from a school: Squiggly was graduated from Stanford.

WELL, I'LL BE HANGED: *HANGED* VERSUS *HUNG*

When you're talking about the past tense, curtains were hung and people were hanged. You can remember that by thinking of "'Twas the night before Christmas": "The stockings were hung by the chimney with care." That's right. Stockings were hung. On the other hand, the standard English word is *hanged* when you are talking about killing people by dangling them from a rope. Therefore, it's correct to say that Saddam Hussein was hanged in Baghdad. To remember *hanged*, I think of a prospector in the Old West expressing surprise by saying, "I'll be hanged!" Hangings were common in the Old West.

It seemed a little curious to me that there would be two past-tense forms of the word *hang* that differ depending on their meaning, so I did a little digging and found out that in Old English there were two different words for *hang* (*hon* and *hangen*), and the entanglement of these words (plus an Old Norse word *hengjan*) is responsible for there being two past-tense forms of the word *hang* today.

IMPACT

Impact has taken root in the business world as a replacement for *affect,* as in *Cutting prices will impact our salespeople.* The problem is that many people object to using *impact* this way; they maintain that it means "to hit" and that any other use is jargon.

Yes, you will find the definition "to influence" in the dictionary under *impact,* but trust me, you'll lead a happier life if you shun such usage.

If I Wanted to Wait Online, I'd Be at My Computer: *In Line* Versus *On Line*

A common regionalism that listeners ask me about is people using the phrase *on line* instead of *in line* to mean they are physically waiting in a row with other people. For example, Mary wrote that she read a story in *The New York Times* describing people standing on line instead of standing in line. She said she's been hearing it more and more in the past few years and thinks it sounds ridiculous, and a listener named Julie noted that it's irritating because when people say they are on line, she assumes they are on the Internet.

There's nothing grammatically incorrect about using *on line* to mean standing in line; it just sounds strange to people who aren't used to hearing it. An online language map from the University of Wisconsin–Milwaukee shows that people who say *on line* are clustered in New York City, New Jersey, Connecticut, Massachusetts, possibly Philadelphia. This is a very small but densely populated, media-rich area. The phrase *standing on line* will probably spread as it becomes widely distributed by New York television programs and publications and as people travel and move in and out of the region.

Today, a Google search for "standing in line" returns about thirty-seven times as many hits as a search for "standing on line," so it would appear that for the time being *in line* is still much more common.

Into the Wild: *Into* Versus *In To*

Into is a preposition that has many definitions, but they all generally relate to direction.

On the other hand, *in* by itself can be an adverb, preposition, or adjective (and *to* by itself is a preposition or an adverb). Sometimes *in* and *to* just end up next to each other.

Maybe examples will help!

He walked into the room.

(Which direction was he going? Into the room.)

We broke in to the room.

("Broke in" is a phrasal verb. What did you break in to? The room.)

SPITEFUL GRAMMAR: *IN SPITE OF* VERSUS *DESPITE*

"In spite of" and "despite" mean the same thing and are interchangeable. For example, it is correct to say either of the following:

She ran well despite having old shoes.

She ran well in spite of having old shoes.

Some people prefer "despite" because it is shorter. ("In despite of" is wrong.)

IT'S HORRIBLE: *IT'S* VERSUS *ITS*

When I was in second grade, I lost a spelling bee because I misspelled the word *its*. I put an apostrophe in when I shouldn't have, and it was a very traumatic moment in my young life. I think this lesson is burned into my mind precisely because of my past misdeeds, and although I can't change my past, I believe the next best thing would be to save all of you from similar apostrophe-induced horrors.

It's with an apostrophe *s always* means "it is" or "it has." For example, you could write, "It's lunch time," with *it*-apostrophe-*s*, or you could write, "It is lunch time," without the contraction. *It's* is a contraction of two words: *it is*.

It's [it is] lunch time.

It's [it is] a shame the chocolate tree is out of season.

Its is the possessive form of *it*. You would use *its* without the apostrophe in sentences like these:

The tree needs its branches trimmed.

The chocolate tree has a scratch on its trunk.

Every time I see the eBay commercials with three-dimensional "its" standing in for products, I flash back to second grade and feel as if the *its* are out to get me. So maybe that odd image of wild crazy *its* chasing Grammar Girl around the room can help you remember to use special care when confronted with *its*. They're very dangerous!

The reason for the confusing *its*-trap is that *its* without an apostrophe is a possessive pronoun just like *hers, ours,* and *yours*. None of the possessive pronouns take an apostrophe *s* to become possessive. You make most words possessive by adding an apostrophe *s* to the end, but not pronouns. *Who* is the other pronoun that can cause apostrophe confusion because it can also exist with or without an apostrophe *s*. That's because *who's* is a contraction for *who is* or *who has*. *Whose* is the possessive form of *who*.

Who's at the door?

Whose door is that?

Just remember to take an extra second to consider whether you are using the right form of *its* and *whose*. Even if you know the difference, it's easy to slip up when you are writing quickly.

WHAT I LIKE ABOUT YOU: *LIKE* VERSUS *AS*

I bet you didn't know there is a raging grammar war about the word *like* (and I'm, like, not even, like, referring to Valley Girl dialect). If you don't believe me, walk into a room full of grammarians, plop down in a comfy chair, and say, "It's *like* I'm sitting in my own living room." I dare you!

The background is that traditionally *like* is a preposition and *as* is a conjunction. Nevertheless, people have been using *like* as if it were a conjunction for at least one hundred years, and grammarians have been raging against that use for just as long.

First, let's quickly review prepositions and conjunctions. Prepositions create relationships between words in a clause or phrase. Examples are *in, around,* and *through.* Note that prepositions are not usually followed by verbs.

Squiggly walked *through* the door.

Aardvark was *in* the loft.

A conjunction connects words, phrases, or clauses. Common conjunctions are *and, but,* and *or.* Note that an entire clause (including a verb) can follow a conjunction.

Squiggly walked through the door *and* caught Aardvark in the loft.

The proper way to differentiate between *like* and *as* is to use *like* when no verb follows.

Squiggly throws like *a raccoon.*

It acted just like *my computer.*

Notice that when I use *like,* the words that come after are generally simple. *A raccoon* and *my computer* are the objects of the preposition.

If the clause that comes next includes a verb, then you should use *as.*

Squiggly throws as *if he were a raccoon.*

He acted just as *I would expect him to behave.*

Notice that when I use *as,* the words that come after tend to be more complex.

You generally hear *like* used in everyday speech, so that helps me remember that *like* is the simpler word—at least it is followed by simpler words. *As* sounds stuffier and is followed by a more complex clause that contains a verb.

Whether you abide by this rule or not probably depends on how much of a grammar stickler you are. It's common to hear sentences like this: *It's like I'm back in high school.* And as a result, many people don't know it's wrong.

I have to admit that after researching this topic I felt a bit brow-beaten. Even as *like* is becoming more entrenched in everyday use, professional grammarians are absolutely resolved that this is a trend worth fighting against. Many language experts seem fully prepared to rail against the conjunctive use of *like* with all their might.

So my advice is don't do it—don't use *like* as a conjunction, especially in writing, unless you are ready for the full force of rampaging grammarians to rain down on you (which is not what I'm generally going for in the advice I give you).

Here are more examples of correct sentences to help you remember the rule:

My cousin looks like *Batman*.

My neighbor yelled like *a maniac*.

It's as if *my cousin were Batman*.

My neighbor yelled as though *he were a maniac*.

A final note is that there is no discernible difference between *as if* and *as though*. Some sources say that *as if* is often used for less likely scenarios—my cousin being Batman—and *as though* for more likely scenarios—my neighbor is a maniac—but this isn't a definitive rule.

Please, Take This Literally: *Literally*

The word *literally* literally means "in a literal sense." Exactly. Without exaggeration. Word for word. When you say your head is going to literally

Squiggly's head is about to *literally* explode.

explode, there are a lot of people whose blood pressure literally rises as they imagine putting lit firecrackers in your ears to make your sentence correct. It's best to avoid using *literally* to add extra emphasis to your writing.

I WISH I MAY, I WISH I MIGHT: *MAY* VERSUS *MIGHT*

The difference between *may* and *might* is subtle. If something is likely to happen, use *may*:

Squiggly may come over later.

Aardvark may get dressed up.

If something is a mighty stretch, use *might*:

Squiggly might win the lottery.

Aardvark might grow wings and fly.

THE PET PEEVE OF HARD-CORE NITPICKERS: NAUSEOUS VERSUS NAUSEATED

Many people say they are nauseous when their stomach is queasy. Using *nauseous* in that way sometimes makes sticklers nauseated because they stick with the rule that *nauseous* means to induce nausea, whereas *nauseated* means you feel sick.

The nauseous fumes permeated the room.

The fumes were nauseating.

We all felt nauseated.

So although only the most irritating people will judge you on your grammar when you're describing how sick you feel, it's best to avoid *nauseous* altogether and use *nauseated* when you're well enough to care about word choice and *nauseating* when you're describing something that makes you sick.

I'M PASSING OUT MEMORY TRICKS: PASSED VERSUS PAST

Past is a noun you use when talking about a long time ago: *that was in the past.*

Passed is a verb you use when talking about going by something: *we passed the store a mile ago.*

My quick and dirty tip for remembering the difference is to make an "ssss" sound when you pass by things (*whossshhh*) to help you remember that the word with two s's is an action. Sure it's silly, and the other people in your car may look at you strangely, but I bet you'll remember, and wouldn't you rather have people question your sanity than your grasp of the English language?

GUILTY AS CHARGED: *PLED* VERSUS *PLEADED*

Can you open a newspaper these days without reading about a star or politician pleading guilty to a crime? I'd guess not, given how many e-mail messages I receive asking about the correct use of the verb *to plead*!

Although *pled* and *pleaded* are both in common use, language sticklers prefer *pleaded*.

> **Squiggly pleaded guilty to stealing the chocolate tree seeds.**

> **Sir Fragalot pleaded guilty to shouting incomplete sentences in the town square.**

A Google News search returns about six hundred entries for "pled guilty" and about thirty-seven thousand entries for "pleaded guilty."

PEOPLE THESE DAYS: *PEOPLE* VERSUS *PERSONS*

Nowadays, *people* is almost always the right choice when you are talking about more than one person.

> **How many people were at the party?**

> **Eight people showed up.**

Some dictionaries don't even include *persons* as the plural of *person* anymore, and most of the dictionaries that do include *persons* note that it is uncommon, archaic, or going out of style. Traditionally, *people* was proper when referring to a mass of people (e.g., Squiggly couldn't believe how many people were at the fair), and *persons* was proper when referring to a distinct number of individuals (e.g., Squiggly noted that eight persons showed up for the meeting).

AND THEN THERE WERE NONE:
THEN VERSUS THAN

Do you get confused about *then* versus *than*? Don't worry; you aren't alone. People ask me about this a lot.

Then has an element of time. For example, it can mean "next" or "at that time":

We ate, and then we went to the movies.

Movies were a lot cheaper back then.

Than conveys a comparison:

DVDs are more expensive than video cassettes.

Aardvark is taller than Squiggly.

The quick and dirty tip is that *than* and *comparison* both have the letter *a* in them, and *then* and *time* both have the letter *e* in them.

WHICH'S BREW: THAT VERSUS WHICH

That versus *which* is covered so frequently in grammar books that I almost hate to bring it up, but using the wrong word is such a common mistake that I feel obligated to cover it. I used to edit documents all the time where people used the wrong word, and what really killed me was when I sent a document to a client for review and got it back with a perfectly fine *that* changed to a *which*.

Here's the deal: some people will argue that the rules are more complex and flexible than this, but I like to make things as simple as possible, so I say that you use *that* before a restrictive clause and *which* before everything else.

A restrictive element is just part of a sentence you can't get rid of because it specifically restricts the noun. Here's an example:

Gems that sparkle often elicit forgiveness.

The words *that sparkle* restrict the kind of gems you're talking about. Without them, the meaning of the sentence would change. Without them, you would be saying that all gems elicit forgiveness, not just the gems that sparkle. (Note also that you don't need commas around the words *that sparkle*.)

A nonrestrictive element is something that can be left off without changing the meaning of the sentence. You can think of a nonrestrictive element as simply additional information. Here's an example:

Diamonds, which are expensive, often elicit forgiveness.

Alas, in Grammar Girl's world, diamonds are always expensive, so leaving out the words *which are expensive* doesn't change the meaning of the sentence. Also note that the phrase is surrounded by commas.

A quick and dirty tip (with apologies to Wiccans and Hermione Granger) is to remember that you can always throw out the "whiches" and no harm will be done. If it would change the meaning to throw out the element, then you need a *that*. For example, do all cars use hybrid technology? Is every leaf green? The answer is no: only some cars have hybrid technology and only some leaves are green. It would change the meaning to throw out the element in the examples below, so you need a *that*. Note also the "that element" isn't surrounded by commas.

Cars *that have hybrid technology* get great gas mileage.

Leaves *that are green* contain chlorophyll.

WHO SAYS GRAMMAR IS EASY?: *THAT* VERSUS *WHO*

The quick and dirty tip is that you use *who* when you are talking about a person and *that* when you are talking about an object. Stick with that rule and you'll be safe.

But, of course, it is also more complicated than that. The who-goes-with-people rule is the conventional wisdom; on the other hand, there is a long history of writers using *that* as a relative pronoun when writing about people. Chaucer did it, for example.

So, it's more of a gray area than some people think, and if you have strong feelings about it, you could make an argument for using *that* when you're talking about people. But my guess is that most people who use *who* and *that* interchangeably do it because they don't know the difference. I don't consider myself a grammar snob—this is quick and dirty grammar, after all—but in this case, I have to take the side of the people who prefer the strict rule. To me, using *that* when you are talking about a person makes them seem less than human. I always think of my friend who would only refer to his new stepmother as "the woman *that* married my father." He was clearly trying to indicate his animosity and you wouldn't want to do that accidentally.

Finally, even if you accept the conventional wisdom, there are some gray areas and strange exceptions. For example, what do you do when you are talking about something animate that isn't human? It can actually go either way. I would never refer to my dog as anything less than *who*, but my fish could probably be a *that*.

One strange exception is that you can use *whose*, which is the possessive form of *who*, to refer to both people and things because English doesn't have a possessive form of *that*. So it's fine to say, "The desk whose top is cluttered with grammar books," even though it is obviously ridiculous to say, "The desk who is made of cherry wood."

So now you understand the details, but you can also remember the quick and dirty rule that *who* goes with people and *that* goes with things.

THERE IS FIREFIGHTERS ON THE SCENE: *THERE IS* VERSUS *THERE ARE*

Newscasters say things such as *There is firefighters on the scene* with shocking frequency because they turn *there is* into the contraction *there's*. I made this mistake in my own show once early on, so I spent a lot of time pondering what made me do it! Obviously, I would never say, "There is firefighters on the scene," but somehow that contraction—*there's*—just rolls off the tongue in a way that *there are* doesn't because of the double *r* sound. Just know that it's a language land mine to watch out for, especially when you are speaking instead of writing.

JUST TRY TO STOP ME FROM GETTING ANNOYED: *TRY AND* VERSUS *TRY TO*

I got really frustrated while researching the difference between *try and* and *try to* because *try and* is obviously wrong but none of my books seemed willing to take a stand. They all said *try and* is an accepted informal idiom that means "try to." They say to avoid *try and* in formal writing, but not to get too worked up about it otherwise. But none of them addressed what bothers me about the phrase *try and,* which is that if you use *and,* as in this example—*I'm going to try and visit Aardvark*—you are separating *trying* and *visiting.* You're describing two things: *trying* and *visiting.* When you use *try to*—*I am going to try to visit Aardvark*—you are using the preposition *to* to link the trying to the visiting.

I may have to put this on my list of pet peeves, and as I've said before, people almost always form pet peeves about things that are style issues or where the rules aren't clear.

YOU'RE MY FAVORITE READER: *YOUR* VERSUS *YOU'RE*

I believe people get *your* and *you're* mixed up for a simple reason: the words sound the same. You have to just remember the difference. *Your* is the possessive form of *you.*

Do these belong to you?

Are these your maracas?

You're is a contraction of two words: *you are*. Remember that an apostrophe can stand in for missing letters, and in this case it stands in for the missing letter *a*. It doesn't save much space, but it does change the phrase from two syllables to one syllable, so I guess it serves an honorable purpose.

You are a talented percussionist.

You're going to be famous someday.

OBJECTIFICATION: SUBJECT VERSUS OBJECT

There are a few word choices that are tricky because before you can choose, you have to determine whether you are talking about the subject or the object of a sentence, so it adds another layer of things you have to remember. Before we get to the word choices in this section, I'm going to explain the difference between a subject and an object. Don't worry. I know it sounds abstract, but it's easy.

If we think about people, the subject of the sentence is the person doing something, and the object of the sentence is having something done to them. If I call Squiggly, then I am the subject, and Squiggly is the object. He is the target of my action: calling.

Still having a hard time remembering? Here's my favorite mnemonic: If I say, "I love you," you are the object of my affection, and *you* is also the object of the sentence (because I am loving you, making me the subject and *you* the object). How's that? I love you. You are the object of my affection and the object of my sentence. It's like a Valentine's Day card and grammar mnemonic all rolled into one.

Lie Down Sally: *Lay* Versus *Lie*

If you exclude the meaning "to tell an untruth" and just focus on the setting/reclining meaning of *lay* and *lie,* then the important distinction is that *lay* requires a direct object and *lie* does not. So, you lie down on the sofa because you are taking an action (and there is no direct object), but you lay the book down on the table because *lay* refers to the book, which is the target of your action (making the book the direct object).

Those examples are in the present tense, so you are talking about doing something now.

Lie down on the sofa!

Lay down your pencil!

Musical Genius and Memory Tricks

For those of you who are thinking "Direct object? Whatever!" I have a few quick and dirty memory tricks.

You can remember that *lie* means "to recline," which is what people do when they lie down. They sound the same: To *lie* is to "rec-*lie*-n." I remember that you use *lay* when you are laying down an object by thinking of the line "Lay it on me." You're laying something (it, the direct object) on me. It's a catchy, silly, 1970s kind of line, so I can remember it and remember that it is correct.

If you're into music, you can remember that both the Eric Clapton song "Lay Down Sally" and the Bob Dylan song "Lay Lady Lay" are wrong. They should be "Lie Down Sally" and "Lie Lady Lie."

To say "Lay down Sally" would imply that someone should grab Sally and lay her down. If Clapton wanted Sally to rest in his arms on her own, the correct line would be "Lie down Sally." These examples are in the present tense. It's pretty easy: you lay something down; people lie down by themselves.

But then everything goes haywire because *lay* is the past tense of *lie*. It's a total nightmare! One of my listeners recommended a great memory trick for this one. He uses the rhyme "Yesterday, down I lay" to remember that the past tense of *lie* is *lay*.

Now I Lay Me Down to Sleep

One reason I believe that people have a hard time remembering to use *lie* to mean "recline" is the children's prayer that includes the line

"Now I lay me down to sleep." The reason the prayer uses *lay* instead of *lie* is in that line you are talking about laying *yourself* down. So you are the object of your own action. Just as you lay a book on the table, you are laying yourself down on the bed.

That kind of sentence construction is unusual, although you will hear it when people talk about doing something to themselves. For example, people do harm to themselves or see themselves in a mirror.

So don't get confused by that prayer. Just remember that *lie* means "recline," if you've got a direct object you've got to lay it on me, and yesterday, down I lay.

Conjugating *Lay* and *Lie*

Lie is an intransitive verb, and *lay* is a transitive verb.

- **Squiggly wanted to lie down.**
- **Please lay the cat in the mud.**

The past tense of *lie* is *lay:*

- **Last week, Squiggly lay down on the floor.**
- **The cat lay in the mud after it rained yesterday.**

The past participle of *lie* is *lain:*

- **Squiggly has lain on the floor for days.**
- **The cat has lain in the mud for hours.**

The present participle of *lie* is *lying:*

- **Squiggly is lying on the floor.**
- **The cat is lying in the mud.**

The past tense of *lay* is *laid:*

- **Last week, I laid the TPS report on your desk.**
- **Aardvark forcefully laid the book on the table.**

The past participle of *lay* is *laid:*

- **I have laid the TPS report on your desk.**
- **Aardvark has forcefully laid the book on the table.**

The present participle of *lay* is *laying*:

- **He is laying the TPS report on your desk as we speak.**
- **Aardvark considered forcefully laying the book on the table.**

Don't feel bad if you can't remember these verb forms right away. Practice will help, and truthfully, I still have to look most of them up every time I use them. It's important to know what you know, and to look up what you don't know because these *are* hard-and-fast rules.

Present Tense	Present Participle	Past Tense	Past Participle
Lay	Laying	Laid	Have laid
Lie	Lying	Lay	Have lain

SIT. STAY. ROLLOVER: *SIT* VERSUS *SET*

The story with *sit* and *set* is similar to the story with *lay* and *lie: set* requires a direct object, *sit* does not. I have a memory trick that may help you remember the difference between the two words. When you're training a dog, you tell her to sit. My first dog's name was Dude and she was a girl, so we would tell her, "Sit, Dude. Sit." And she would plop her little bottom down. She was a good dog. She was a bullmastiff, so actually her bottom wasn't that little.

So get an image in your mind of a big bullmastiff responding to the command "Sit." That is how you use *sit*—for the action of sitting.

Set, on the other hand, requires an object. I would set Dude's leash on the table, but she would still think we were going for a walk. I know she saw me set it down, but she was always full of hope. In those examples, the leash and the word *it* were the objects. I set *the leash* on the table, and she saw me set *it* down.

So remember that a dog (or person) sits, and you set things, like leashes, down.

Dude, sit!

I wish Dude would sit on her bed instead of on my bed.

If I set her leash on the table, maybe she'll forget about going for a walk.

She saw me set it down, but she still thinks we're going.

WHOM DO YOU LOVE?: *WHO* VERSUS *WHOM*

You've always wondered how to use *who* and *whom*. I know you have! Maybe you don't sit on a grassy hill under an oak tree fondly wondering, but when you have to write a sentence that may need a *whom*, your blood pressure rises at least a degree or two.

I'll have a quick and dirty trick for you later, but first I want you to actually understand the right way to use these words. The words *who* and *whom* are both pronouns. Knowing which word to choose also requires you to know the difference between subject and object because you use *who* when you are referring to the subject of a clause and *whom* when you are referring to the object of a clause.

For example, it is, "Whom did you step on?" if you are trying to figure out that I squished Squiggly because Squiggly is having the squishing done to him. He is the object. Similarly, you could ask me, "Whom do you love?" because you are asking about the object—the target of my love. I know, it's shocking, but George Thorogood and the Destroyers were being grammatically incorrect when they belted out the song, "Who do you love?" It doesn't sound as catchy, but it should have been "Whom do you love?"

So, when is it OK to use *who*? If you were asking about the subject of these sentences then you would use *who*.

Who loves you?

Who stepped on Squiggly?

In both these cases the one you are asking about is the subject—the one taking action—so you use *who*.

Now, back to that blood pressure. I'm not a doctor, and I don't play one on TV, but I can still don my metaphorical white coat and dispense a prescription to lower your blood pressure: it's a simple memory trick—we'll call it the "him-lich" maneuver. It's as easy as testing your sentence with the word *him:* if you can hypothetically answer your question with the word *him,* you need a *whom.*

Here's an example: *who/whom do you love?* Imagine a guy you love—your father, your boyfriend, Chef Boyardee. I'm not here to judge you. The answer to the question *Who/whom do you love?* would be "I love him." You've got a *him,* so the answer is *whom: whom do you love?*

I hope this isn't the first time you've realized that you shouldn't rely on George Thorogood and the Destroyers for grammar guidance.

Remember: *him* equals *whom.*

Whoever Versus Whomever

You can't always use the *him* trick for *whoever* and *whomever,* but the same grammar rule holds true: you use *whoever* when you are talking about the subject (someone taking an action). In the next sentence, *whoever* (the person leaving the doughnuts) is taking the action.

- **Whoever left these doughnuts in the conference room made our day.**

You use *whomever* when you are talking about the object of a sentence, or the person who had something done to them. In the next sentence, *whomever* is the target of my action (seeing them).

- **Whomever I see first will win the tickets.**

Chapter 2
GRAMMAR GIRL ON GRAMMAR

I LOVE WRITING ABOUT USAGE, but basic grammar is something you need to know too. Grammar is the set of rules for putting together a sentence. I think of grammar as the rules to the game of writing. Grammar dictates that an adjective modifies a noun and that singular nouns need singular verbs—stuff like that. (I do touch on some points of grammar in other chapters, but we're going to get into the nitty-gritty rules here.) So without further ado, let's start with some of the common grammar myths.

I'VE GOT A PREPOSITION FOR YOU

Just as Harry Potter was unfairly labeled "undesirable number one" in *Harry Potter and the Deathly Hallows,* ending a sentence with a preposition is often unfairly labeled "undesirable grammar construction number one" by people who were taught that prepositions have a proper place in the world, and it's not at the end of a sentence.

I'm going to start calling this "grammar myth number one" because nearly all grammarians agree that it's fine to end sentences with prepositions, at least in some cases.

So before I lose you, let's back up. What is a preposition?

A preposition is a word that creates a relationship between other words. It's been said that prepositions often deal with space and time,* which always makes me think of *Star Trek.* For example, the prepositions *above, by,* and *over* all say something about a position in space; the prepositions *before, after,* and *since* all say something about time.

Here's an example of a sentence that can end with a preposition:

I hope he cheers up.

A key point, you might say the quick and dirty tip, is that the sentence doesn't work if you leave off the preposition. If you write, "I hope he cheers," it has a completely different meaning from *I hope he cheers up.* Because it has a specific meaning, *cheer up* is actually what's called a "phrasal verb"—a set of words that act as a single verb unit. Phrasal verbs can have a different meaning from the way the words are used individually. For example, the verb *cheer up* specifically means to become happier, not to shout joyfully. So given that *cheer up* is a unit—a phrasal verb—some people don't believe you've ended a sentence with a preposition when you say, "I hope he cheers up." They say you've ended the sentence with a phrasal verb.

Here's a slightly different example of a sentence that can end with a preposition:

What did you step on?

---

* R. Huddleston and G. K. Pullman, *A Student's Introduction to English Grammar* (Cambridge: Cambridge University Press, 2006), pp. 20, 137–38.

You can't say, "What did you step?" You need to say, "What did you step *on*?" to make a proper sentence. Again, if you leave off the *on*, the sentence doesn't make sense, but this time I can hear some of you gnashing your teeth, while thinking, "What about saying, 'On what did you step?'"

But really, have you ever heard anyone talk that way? I've read long, contorted arguments from noted grammarians about why it's OK to end sentences with prepositions when the prepositions aren't extraneous, but the driving point still seems to be that nobody in their right mind talks this way. Yes, you could say, "On what did you step?" but not even grammarians think you should.

But don't get carried away. You can't *always* end sentences with prepositions. When you could leave off the preposition and it wouldn't change the meaning, you should leave it off. Here's an example of a sentence you will hear often if you're listening for it:

Where is she at? (wrong)

Oh, the horror! That is one of the instances where it's not OK to end a sentence with a preposition! The problem is that the sentence *Where is she at?* doesn't need the preposition. *Where is she?* means the same thing, so the *at* is unnecessary.

The problem with unnecessary prepositions doesn't just happen at the ends of sentences. People often throw extraneous prepositions into the middle of sentences, and they shouldn't. Instead of saying, "Squiggly jumped *off of the dock*," it's better to say, "Squiggly jumped *off the dock*." You see? You don't need to say *off of the dock*; *off the dock* says the same thing without the preposition.

To get back to the main point—ending sentences with prepositions—the bottom line is that many people think it's wrong, so I wouldn't advise ending sentences with prepositions in critical situations; for example, you shouldn't do it in a cover letter. I always say, "It's better to be employed than right," at least when it comes to silly grammar myths. But once you're hired, end away, and do your part to dispel grammar myth number one.

Idioms

Idioms are phrases that don't mean what they literally say, but have meaning to native speakers. For example, the phrase *under the weather* is known by most native English speakers to mean that someone isn't feeling well, but if you weren't a native English speaker, you would probably have no idea what *under the weather* means by just looking at the words. I can imagine foreigners trying to figure out what it means to be literally under the weather. They could guess that someone is getting rained on, and who could blame them?

Sometimes idioms break grammar rules too. For example, if you're feeling groovy you could recommend a restaurant or club by saying, "It's where it's at, man." Although *where it's at* violates the true rule about not ending a sentence with a preposition—leave it off if it doesn't change the meaning—it's considered an idiomatic phrase, a saying from the '60s that means something is hip, cool, and trendy, and has nothing to do with its location.

People wonder where idioms come from, and to me a lot of idioms seem to be holdovers of phrases that had a more literal meaning in the past. For example, *Mind your p's and q's* might originate from the way pubs did their bookkeeping many years ago. In another example, some sources say *under the weather* originates from a time when it was more common to travel by boat; during storms seasick passengers would go belowdecks, where the rocking was less intense, and they were literally under the weather that was occurring above deck. However, idioms don't always have such clear historical sources, and even in this case there is disagreement: some sources say *under the weather* simply refers to the belief that bad weather can make you sick.

I WANT TO SPLIT INFINITIVES

I consider it my calling to dispel the myth that it's against the rules to split infinitives. It's fine to split infinitives, and sometimes, I split them when I don't have to just to maliciously make a point. Yeah, that's my idea of fun! I know it may come as a surprise, but Grammar Girl isn't that adventurous.

To understand this "rule," we first have to clearly define the word *infinitive*. An infinitive is just a fancy name for a specific form of a verb. In English, there are two kinds of infinitives: full infinitives and bare infinitives. Bare infinitives are the kinds of verbs you usually see in a dictionary, such as

- Go
- Make
- Run
- Define
- Split
- Break up (phrasal verb)

On the other hand, full infinitives are made up of two or more words, often by putting the word *to* in front of the bare verb. For example

- To go
- To make
- To run
- To define
- To split
- To break up

The logic behind the nineteenth-century rule about not splitting infinitives rests on comparing English to Latin because in Latin there are no two-word infinitives. They don't have to deal with full verbs versus bare verbs. Therefore, it's impossible to split infinitives in Latin. For some reason, many grammarians in the nineteenth century got the notion that because it is impossible to split infinitives in Latin, it shouldn't be done in English either.

But notions change over time, and today almost everyone agrees that it is OK to split infinitives, especially when you would have to change the meaning of the sentence or go through writing gymnastics to avoid the split. English isn't Latin, after all.

Here's an example of a sentence with a split infinitive:

Squiggly decided <u>to</u> quickly <u>remove</u> Aardvark's cats.

In this case, the word *quickly* splits the infinitive *to remove: to <u>quickly</u> remove*.

If you try to unsplit the verb, you actually change the meaning. For example, you might try to say

Squiggly decided quickly <u>to remove</u> Aardvark's cats.

Now, instead of saying Squiggly quickly removed Aardvark's cats (zip zip) while Aardvark stepped out for a minute, you're saying he quickly made the decision to remove the cats.

You could rewrite the sentence without the split infinitive to make the same point. For example

Squiggly decided to grab Aardvark's cats and set them free before Aardvark got back from the corner market.

And that could even be a better sentence (I like the imagery), but from a grammatical standpoint, rewriting isn't necessary. The bottom line is that you can usually avoid splitting infinitives if you want to, but there's no reason to go out of your way to avoid it, and certainly don't let anyone tell you that it's forbidden.

And here's a bonus: If you want to remember what a split infinitive is, just remember what may be the most famous example: *Star Trek*'s "to boldly go where no man has gone before." *To <u>boldly</u> go* is a split infinitive. (As you've probably gathered by now, I'm a *Star Trek* fan—*Star Trek: The Next Generation* was my favorite series, followed by *Star Trek: Deep Space Nine*.)

IRREGULAR VERBS

Since we're talking about verbs, what's up with irregular verbs like *dreamt, went,* and *flung*? Why aren't they *dreamed, goed,* and *flinged*?

To infinitives and beyond!

Regular verbs follow a pattern: you make them past tense by adding -*d* or -*ed*.

present tense	**past tense**
verb	verbd or verbed

Irregular verbs don't follow this pattern; they are holdovers from language past. Believe it or not, conjugation rules were even more complicated in days gone by. Over time, conjugation rules got simpler and most verbs were regularized. Today, English has fewer than two hundred irregular verbs, but some of the most common English verbs are irregular:

present tense	past tense
am	was
go	went
do	did
sit	sat
run	ran
say	said
see	saw

Researchers recently found that the more frequently a verb is used, the less likely it is to be regular. The theory is that it is harder to change a word that people use every day than one that isn't so integral to everyday life. Be sure to look at the appendix on page 199 for other common irregular verbs.

People who grew up speaking English just know the irregular verbs (although children often get them wrong—How many times have you heard a toddler say, "We goed to the store"?), but for the most part, people who are learning English have to memorize them.

Some additional verb confusion is caused by the differences that exist between British and American English—people speaking British English tend to use more irregular verbs than people speaking American English. For example, *dreamt, learnt,* and *spilt* are the common past tense verbs in Britain, whereas *dreamed, learned,* and *spilled* are the common forms in the United States.

THE SINGLE LIFE: *THEY* AS A SINGULAR PRONOUN

Let's say you're writing a sentence that starts *When a student suc-ceeds.* . . . At that point there's enormous confusion about how you should finish the sentence when you're talking about one unknown person:

he **should thank** *his* **teacher**

she **should thank** *her* **teacher**

he or she should thank *his or her* teacher
they should thank *their* teacher

Betty, one of my listeners, summed it up best by saying, "*He or she* seems too awkward, *he* seems sexist, and *one* seems archaic." I would add that exclusively using *she* also seems sexist, the hybrid *s/he* seems silly and awkward, the various alternative pronouns people have suggested (*e, sie, ze,* etc.) will never catch on, and switching between *he* and *she* is downright confusing to readers. A listener named Bryan called switching between *he* and *she* "whiplash grammar," which I love.

Then there's the solution that everyone loves to hate: using the personal pronoun *they,* which breaks the rule that you don't use a plural pronoun with a singular antecedent.

Honestly, I don't think there is a perfect solution, and I've been avoiding the question because I know that no matter what I say I'm going to make someone angry. But then Ken from Denver wrote in pleading for help. He had obviously spent a lot of time looking through *The Chicago Manual of Style* and had concluded that their answer is "My, that's a toughie. Try to avoid it." I agree that an answer like that is unhelpful, so I decided to muster up some courage and try to do better.

First, some of you might disagree that using *he* is sexist; but even if you disagree, you should still at least consider the alternatives because the major style guides recommend against using *he* in a generic way.

When I am confronted with this problem, I first take the *Chicago* route and ask if there is any way to avoid the problem. Usually this involves simply making the original noun plural. You could say, "When students [plural] succeed, they should thank their teacher." Sometimes more extensive rewriting is required, and if necessary, I'll do it. I would rewrite a whole paragraph if it meant I could avoid the problem.

Rewriting is almost always possible, but if it isn't, then you have to make a choice. If I'm writing a formal document, I'll use *he or she.* For example, *He or she accidentally knocked over a water bottle.* Admittedly, it's a little awkward, but if you're already using formal language, I don't think it's too distracting.

I will state for the record that I am a firm believer that someday *they* will be the acceptable choice for this situation. English currently lacks a word that fits the bill, and many people are already either mistakenly or purposefully using *they* as a singular gender-neutral pronoun, so it seems logical that rules will eventually move in that direction.

Nevertheless, it takes a bold, confident, and possibly reckless person to use *they* with a singular antecedent today. I could almost feel people's blood pressure rising as I started to imply that it is OK to use *they*.

The thing is, if you are a respected editor in charge of writing a style guide for your entire organization, you can get away with making it acceptable to use *they* with a singular antecedent. I would even encourage you to do so, and there are a variety of credible references that will back you up including the *Random House Dictionary* and *Fowler's Modern English Usage*. You would be in the company of revered authors such as Jane Austen, Lewis Carroll, and Shakespeare. But, if you are responsible to superiors, there's a good chance that at least one of them will think you are careless or ignorant if you use *they* with a singular antecedent.

So here's the quick and dirty tip: rewrite your sentences to avoid the problem. If that's not possible, check if the people you are writing for have a style guide. If not, use *he or she* if you want to play it safe, or use *they* if you feel bold and prepared to defend yourself.

Grammar by Committee

Generic pronouns are a very contentious area of language, and Grammar Girl listeners are split in their opinions. In a completely unscientific website poll with about twelve hundred respondents, 40 percent of respondents preferred *his or her*, 32 percent preferred *their*, and 25 percent preferred *his* in the sentence *A student should thank___teacher.*

IF I ONLY HAD A BRAIN: MISPLACED MODIFIERS

Simple Misplaced Modifiers

Of all the writing errors you can make, misplaced modifiers are among the most likely to confuse your readers, but they're also kind of fun because misplaced modifiers can give your sentences silly meanings that you never intended. If you're not careful, you can end up writing that your boss *is* a corn muffin instead of that your boss *invested in* corn muffins.

I once worked with an editor who liked to send everyone in the office especially hilarious sentences that contained misplaced modifiers. We produced enough reports to keep two copy editors busy, and many of the writers were scientists, so there were always lots of opportunities to find misplaced modifiers. The e-mailed examples were entertaining, unless you were the one who had written the offending sentence.

Modifiers are just what they sound like—words or phrases that modify something else. Misplaced modifiers are modifiers that modify something you didn't intend them to modify. For example, the word *only* is a modifier that's easy to misplace.

These two sentences mean different things:

Squiggly ate *only* chocolate.

Squiggly *only ate* chocolate.

The first sentence (*Squiggly ate only chocolate*) means that Squiggly ate nothing but chocolate—no fruit, no meat, just chocolate.

The second sentence (*Squiggly only ate chocolate*) means that all Squiggly did with chocolate was eat it. He didn't buy, melt, or sell it. He only ate it.

It's easiest to get modifiers right when you keep them as close as possible to the thing they are modifying. When you're working with one-word modifiers, for example, they usually go right before the word they modify.

Here's another example of two sentences with very different meanings:

Aardvark *almost failed* every art class he took.

Aardvark failed *almost every art class* he took.

The first sentence (*Aardvark almost failed every art class he took*) means that although it was close, he passed all those classes.

The second sentence (*Aardvark failed almost every art class he took*) means that he passed only a few art classes.

Note again that the modifier, *almost,* acts on what directly follows it: *almost failed* versus *almost every class.* In either case, Aardvark is probably not going to make a living as a painter, but these two sentences mean different things.

A similar rule applies when you have a short phrase at the beginning of a sentence: whatever the phrase refers to should immediately follow the comma. Here's an example:

Rolling down the hill, Squiggly was frightened that the rocks would land on the campsite.

In that sentence, it's Squiggly, not the rocks, rolling down the hill because the word *Squiggly* is what comes immediately after the modifying phrase, *rolling down the hill.*

To fix that sentence, I could write, "Rolling down the hill, the rocks threatened the campsite and frightened Squiggly." Or I could write, "Squiggly was frightened that the rocks, which were rolling down the hill, would land on the campsite."

Here's another funny sentence:

Covered in wildflowers, Aardvark pondered the hillside's beauty.

In that sentence, Aardvark, not the hillside, is covered with wildflowers because the word *Aardvark* is what comes directly after the modifying phrase, *covered in wildflowers.*

If I want Aardvark to ponder a wildflower-covered hillside, I need to

Covered in wildflowers, Aardvark   Covered in wildflowers, the hillside
pondered the hillside's beauty.   inspired Aardvark with its beauty.

write something like, "Covered in wildflowers, the hillside struck Aard-vark with its beauty."

Here, the words *the hillside* immediately follow the modifying phrase, *covered in wildflowers.*

Or better yet, I could write, "Aardvark pondered the beauty of the wildflowers that covered the hillside."

I can think of even more ways to write the sentence, but the point is to be careful with introductory statements: they're often a breeding ground for misplaced modifiers, so make sure they are modifying what you intend.

Modifiers are hilarious! (Grammar Girl is easily amused.) In addition to misplacing modifiers, you can dangle them and make them squint!

It's a Dangler: Dangling Modifiers

A "dangling modifier" describes something that isn't even in your sentence. Usually you are implying the subject and taking for granted that your reader will know what you mean—not a good strategy. Here's an example:

Hiking the trail, the birds chirped loudly.

The way the sentence is written, the birds are hiking the trail because they are the only subject present in the sentence. If that's not what you mean, you need to rewrite the sentence to something like, "Hiking the trail, Squiggly and Aardvark heard birds chirping loudly."

Hey, Squinty: Squinty Modifiers

And how do you make a modifier squint? By placing it between two things that it could reasonably modify, meaning the reader has no idea which one to choose.

Children who laugh, rarely are shy.

As written, that sentence could mean two different things: children who rarely laugh are shy, or children who laugh are rarely shy.

In the original sentence (*Children who laugh rarely are shy*) the word *rarely* is squinting between the words *laugh* and *are shy*. I think "shifty modifier" would be a better name, but I don't get to name these things, so they are called squinting modifiers (or sometimes they are also called two-way modifiers).

So remember to be careful when using modifiers; they are easily misplaced, dangled, and made to squint. My theory is that these problems arise because you know what you mean to say, so the humor of the errors doesn't jump out at you. Misplaced modifiers often crop up in first drafts and are easily noticed and remedied when you reread your work the next day.

He Was Completely Dead: Modifying Absolutes

While we're on the topic of modifiers, there's another thing people often do with them that isn't kosher: modify words with absolute meanings such as *dead* and *unique*. (In formal language terms, such words are considered "nongradable.")

That is the most unique painting I've ever seen. (wrong)

The issue is that the primary meaning of *unique* is "one of a kind"; it's an absolute, so something can't be more unique than something else. Here's the deal: most authoritative sources say it's bad to qualify or compare the word *unique,* and then in the next breath they all acknowledge that it's commonly done, and that it's been done for a long time.

For example, *Fowler* would consider *unique* to be weakened in the sentence *Those are very unique maracas.* His book states, "It must be conceded that *unique* is losing its quality of being not gradable (or absolute)," but he also notes that it continues to be controversial.

According to the *Oxford English Dictionary,* since the middle of the nineteenth century *unique* has "had a tendency to take the wider meaning of *uncommon, unusual, remarkable.*"

A lot of usage notes talk about the role advertising plays in diluting the meaning of *unique.* The notes made me laugh because I have a friend who sells new homes, and I recently gave her a hard time after she made a sign advertising her "unique" new subdivision. I used to live in one of those subdivisons, so I'm not knocking them, but you can get lost because all the houses look alike. They are anything but unique, and her sign cracked me up.

It seems to me that the trend toward talking about degrees of uniqueness is an example of how language changes. I had to ask myself if I am on the side of sticking with the older rule or going with common usage, and in this case I believe *unique* should continue to mean one of a kind. There are plenty of other words people can use to talk about degrees. A piece of art can be the most stunning painting you've ever seen, or the marimbas can be very unusual. There's just no reason to assign a new meaning to *unique*. So it's good to know that this is a controversial area of language, but I can't recommend modifying absolute words with qualifiers in phrases such as *very unique* and *completely dead*.

IF I WERE A RICH GIRL: SUBJUNCTIVE VERBS

Whether you prefer Tevye's version from *Fiddler on the Roof* or Gwen Stefani's more recent interpretation, *If I were a rich man/girl* is a classic example of a sentence in the subjunctive mood.

You see, verbs can be as moody as teenage girls. Yes, before the Internet and before emoticons, somebody already thought that it was important to communicate moods. So, like many other languages, English verbs can have moods ranging from commanding (imperative mood) to matter-of-fact (indicative mood) to doubtful or wishful (subjunctive mood). The mood of the verb *to be,* when you use the phrase *I were,* is called the subjunctive mood.

Hundreds of years ago subjunctive verbs were quite common, but in modern English their use is rare, with *I were* being one of the few examples left that doesn't sound archaic to our modern ears.

A subjunctive verb is used to communicate feelings such as wishfulness, hopefulness, or imagination—things that aren't real or true. For example, in the song "If I Were a Rich Man" Tevye is fantasizing about all the things he would do if he were rich. He's not rich, he's just imagining, so *if I were* is the correct statement. *I were* often follows the word *if,* because *if* usually means you are wishing or imagining.

In a subjunctive sentence the verb is often also followed by a statement using wishful words like *would* or *could.* For example, again from *Fiddler on the Roof*, "*If I were* a wealthy man . . . I *wouldn't* have to work hard."

A MILLION LITTLE FRAGMENTS: SENTENCE FRAGMENTS

I often imagine that my listeners and readers are writing articles and essays and books, but I was recently reminded that some people make their living writing shorter things like headlines and ad copy, and that it's really hard work.

When writers focus too much on brevity, sometimes they leave out important words and produce fragments instead of sentences. Unfortunately, you can't magically make any set of words a sentence by starting with a capital letter and ending with a period (or an exclamation point). Most sentences have at least one subject and one verb.

A verb is an action word that tells the reader what's happening, and a subject does the action of the verb. You can make a complete sentence with just two words: *Squiggly hurried. Squiggly,* our beloved snail, is the subject, and *hurried* is the verb.

There's even a sentence form called the imperative that lets you make one-word sentences such as *Run!* Imperative sentences are commands, and the subject is always assumed to be the person you are talking to. If Squiggly looks at Aardvark and says, "Run!," Aardvark knows that he's the one who should be running. It's such a strong command that he knows it is imperative for him to run.

You can also make a one-word sentence using an exclamation. For example, *Ouch! Wow! Eureka!*

So you can make imperative sentences such as *Run!* with one verb, and exclamatory sentences with one exclamation or interjection such as *Ouch!* or *Hello!*, and you can make simple complete sentences such as *Squiggly hurried* with a subject and a verb. But there is also a case where you have a subject and a verb, but you still don't have a complete sentence. Ack! This happens when your fragment is a dependent clause, meaning that it depends on the other part of the sentence: the main clause. If you're dependent on your parents, then you need them. It's the same with dependent clauses; they need their main clauses.

Dependent clause fragments usually start with a subordinating conjunction such as *because, although,* or *if.* I'm going to need more examples to explain this one. It makes a lot more sense when you see examples.

Let's go back to our simple sentence: *Squiggly hurried.* I'm sure you all get that *Squiggly hurried* is a complete sentence because it has a subject and a verb, but look what happens if you put a subordinating conjunction in front of it: *Because Squiggly hurried.* By adding *because,* I've messed up the sentence; now I need something to explain the *because.* The *because* makes the whole thing a dependent clause that can't exist on its own. (Well, it can exist, but it's a fragment and that's bad.) The dependent clause now makes sense only if it has a main clause; for example, *Aardvark was relieved because Squiggly hurried.*

To sum up, there are some easy tests to see if you have a fragment. The easiest test is to ask yourself if there is a verb. If there's no verb, then it's probably a fragment. Then, if there is just one word, ask yourself if the sentence is an exclamation, an interjection, or a command. If it's not, then it's a fragment. Finally, ask yourself if it is a subordinate clause to the previous sentence. If it is, then it is a fragment. That last one is a little trickier, but I'm sure you can do it!

Can't We All Just Get Along: Subject-Verb Agreement

Singular nouns take singular verbs and plural nouns take plural verbs. It's really quite simple.

I am happy.

We are happy.

But wait! A few tricky words might cause you to doubt yourself.

Everyone Hates Subject-Verb Agreement

Everyone sounds like a lot of people, but in grammar land, *everyone* is a singular noun and takes a singular verb:

Everyone is happy. (right)

Everyone are happy. (wrong)

Everyone and *everybody* mean the same thing and are interchangeable, so *everybody* takes a singular verb too. The same rules hold true for *anyone* and *anybody,* and *no one* and *nobody*—they're singular and interchangeable. (In Britain, these words are sometimes considered plural.)

Playing with the Band

Band names (and team names) are generally plural in the United States, but they are generally singular in Britain. Some people go by the rule that if the name sounds plural (like *The Beatles* and *Black Eyed Peas*), they treat it as plural, and if it sounds singular (like *Lifehouse* or *Coldplay*), they treat it as singular.

Let's Take Up a Collection

Collective nouns are words such as *team, family, orchestra,* and *board;* they are nouns that describe a group. Again, they sound like a lot of people, but they are usually singular nouns (in the United States).

The family is going on vacation next week.

The orchestra plays on Thursdays.

Some collective nouns, such as *couple,* are considered plural if each person has a sense of individuality. (I know that is terribly vague, but it's the rule.) For example, you would say, "The couple are vacationing separately this year," because there is a sense that it is two individual people; but you would say, "Each couple is going to Bermuda on a different week," because each couple is being spoken of as a unit. You just have to use your best judgment, and even though this seems tricky, the good news is that you can never really get it wrong because (1) there is no real rule, and (2) you can always just assert that you were thinking of the couple as individuals (or a unit) if someone questions your verb choice.

Since we started with an example from *Star Trek,* I'll end with an example from *Star Trek* too! To remember that collective nouns are usually singular, think of the Borg. (For the uninitiated, the Borg is a group of cyborgs who don't have a sense of individuality and instead act as a "collective.") With the Borg, the group is one, a singular collective—just as collective nouns are usually singular.

Chapter 3
LET'S GET IT STARTED:
STARTING A SENTENCE

NOW THAT YOU'VE MASTERED usage and basic grammar, it's time to start writing. But argg! Writer's block is bad enough without having to worry about the nitpicky little "rules" governing how you should start a sentence. *And, but, however, because*—it's enough to make you click that Solitaire/Bejeweled/Second Life/YouTube button (you know the one) and procrastinate for one more day.

I have good news: you can forget almost every rule you think you know about how not to start a sentence (unless you're writing a cover letter—then you should see the "Idiot Manager" box at the end of this chapter). Sometimes how you start a sentence matters in formal settings, but many dictums are only delusions.

STARTING A SENTENCE WITH *HOWEVER*

When people ask me about the sentence-starting rules, *however* is the word they mention most often. Rest assured: it's fine to use *however* at the beginning of a sentence; you just need to know when to use a comma.

The comma is important because *however* is a conjunctive adverb that can be used in two different ways: it can be a conjunction that joins main clauses, or it can be an adverb that modifies a clause.

"What is an adverb?" you ask. Most commonly, it is a word that modifies a verb. That's easy to remember because *adverb* has the word *verb* in it. Adverbs often end in *-ly. Quickly* is an adverb in this sentence: *Squiggly ran quickly. Quickly* describes how Squiggly ran. Adverbs can also modify adjectives, other adverbs, clauses, and whole sentences. A conjunctive adverb is a transitional word that joins two clauses that could be independent sentences, and it provides meaning about the relationship between the two sentences. Examples include *however, therefore,* and *nevertheless.* (See the appendix on page 196 for more examples.)

If you start a sentence with *however* and don't follow it with a comma, *however* means "in whatever manner" or "to whatever extent."

However Squiggly tried, he couldn't get his mind off chocolate.

However loud the maracas, they couldn't drown out the sound of the gathering peeves.

In both of those sentences, *however* isn't acting like a conjunction. It's not joining anything to anything else. I don't believe anyone has ever disputed starting a sentence with *however* when it's used this way.

On the other hand, the esteemed grammarians Strunk and White did say in their book, *The Elements of Style,* that you shouldn't start a sentence with *however* when you mean "nevertheless" or "on the other hand." Brace yourself. I'm going to dis Strunk and White, but only because other grammarians did it first. (I have the heart of a field mouse.)

Most of the time people stick with Strunk and White, but everyone who's anyone in modern grammatical society (don't you wish you could come to our parties?) has decided that the classic advice is unreasonable.

Here's why: when you put a comma after *however* at the beginning of a sentence, everyone knows it means "nevertheless." There's no reason to outlaw a perfectly reasonable use of the word when you can solve the problem with a comma!

> **Squiggly couldn't forget about chocolate. *However,* he wasn't trying very hard.**

> **Squiggly was Aardvark's best friend. *However,* sometimes Aardvark found him exasperating.**

Take that Strunk. Take that White. Please don't haunt me. More famous writers than I have defied your directive; go haunt them if you're feeling peeved.

If you have an unhealthy reverence for Mr. Strunk or Mr. White and want to avoid starting a sentence with *however,* it's not hard to do—the quick and dirty tip is to grab a semicolon and use it to connect your two main clauses instead of separating them with a period.

> **Squiggly was Aardvark's best friend. *However,* sometimes Aardvark found him exasperating.**

> **Squiggly was Aardvark's best friend; however, sometimes Aardvark found him exasperating.**

Treat the other conjunctive adverbs the same way. For example, if *indeed* is used in the middle of two independent clauses as a connector, treat it as you would *however*—put a semicolon before it and a comma after.

> **Squiggly was Aardvark's best friend; *indeed,* sometimes Aardvark thought Squiggly was his only friend.**

You can also bury a *however* that means "nevertheless," "on the other hand," etc., in the middle of a sentence. You might do this to avoid using it at the beginning when you suspect your audience contains rabid Strunk and White fans, or you might do it because it makes sense with the rhythm of your sentence. When you put *however* in the middle of a sentence like this, it should be surrounded by commas.

Friendship, however, is a complicated dance.

A gift of chocolate, however, has the power to salve minor missteps.

Again, put a comma before and after *however* when you use it in the middle of a sentence that way. People often get confused about this point because in long sentences sometimes you need a comma and sometimes you need a semicolon with your *however*. Just remember that you only use the semicolon when you are joining two main clauses and the *however* just happens to be in the way, shouting "nevertheless." Just think of a semicolon as a sentence splicer—it splices together two main clauses.

So don't let anyone tell you it's wrong to start a sentence with *however*. On the other hand, it may be a good idea to avoid the practice if you're applying for a job since a lot of people mistakenly believe it's wrong. Mind your commas and semicolons, and don't use any punctuation after *however* when you use it to mean "in whatever manner" or "to whatever extent."

STARTING A SENTENCE WITH *HOPEFULLY*

If you believe *hopefully* is a sentence adverb, and you don't care what people think of you, you can start a sentence with *hopefully*.

Frankly, I can't do it. If you've ever heard me give a radio interview, you've probably heard me self-correct. I'll start a sentence, "Hopefully, the interrobang . . . ," panic [Screech. Internal panic. Holy cats, I just started a sentence with "hopefully." Abort! Abort!], and start over. "I HOPE the interrobang gets its own key on the keyboard someday."

If you read the definition of adverb in the "However" section, you might have noticed that adverbs can modify whole sentences. When they do this they are called (unimaginatively) sentence adverbs. (Adverbs are starting to bug me because they can't decide what their job is. How would you feel if I suddenly threw in a chapter on gardening or genetic engineering? But I digress.)

Here are some examples of less controversial sentence adverbs in action:

Fortunately, the peeves were upwind.

Honestly, I wish I were somewhere else.

Hopefully, you can see that [Screech. Panic.] . . . I am hopeful you can see that the sentence adverbs *fortunately* and *honestly* modify the whole sentence. *Fortunately* relates to the entire point that the peeves were upwind, and *honestly* describes the subject's state of mind and gives the whole sentence a confessional quality.

The *Oxford English Dictionary* shows the first use of *hopefully* as a sentence adverb meaning "I hope" in 1932, so it is relatively new, as far as words go. For the three hundred years before 1932, *hopefully* primarily meant "in a hopeful manner," and this is still the more acceptable use today.

Squiggly looked *hopefully* in the direction of the chocolate tree.

Hopefully, he broached the subject of an expedition.

"Ah ha!," the holdover* language sticklers will say as they read that second example. "We've got you now! 'Hopefully, he broached the subject of an expedition' could mean two different things. It could mean he broached the subject in a hopeful manner, or it could mean the storyteller

---

* Many language experts have come around on starting a sentence with *hopefully*. The response ranges from an enthusiastic "fully standard" by Dictionary.com to a resigned "lost cause" from Bryan Garner, author of *Garner's Modern American Usage*.

is hopeful that he broached the subject of an expedition." And the language sticklers are right.

The counterargument is that there are few instances where a reasonable person would be confused; context usually makes the meaning clear. And if there is an instance where intolerable confusion will ensue if you start a sentence with *hopefully,* don't do it. There's no reason to throw the baby out with the bathwater. In most cases, the meaning is clear:

> **Hopefully, the book will do well.**
>
> **Hopefully, it won't rain.**
>
> **We don't have chips to go with the salsa? Hopefully, Aardvark is getting chips on his way home.**

Now, although I've made a strong argument for starting a sentence with *hopefully,* my advice is this: don't do it.

For some reason, to many language sticklers, starting a sentence with *hopefully* has become a mark of ignorance. It's not as bad as using *literally* for emphasis when you mean "figuratively" or saying someone "graduated college," but it won't help you win friends or influence people.

I am hopeful that starting a sentence with *hopefully* will become more acceptable in the future. For a list of sentence adverbs that are always acceptable, see the appendix on page 195.

STARTING A SENTENCE WITH *BECAUSE* (AND OTHER SUBORDINATING CONJUNCTIONS)

Because is a subordinating conjunction—when it begins a clause, that clause is dependent on the main clause in the sentence. As I said in the section on sentence fragments, dependent clauses need their main clauses just as kids need their parents.

For grade-school children, subordinating conjunctions are only slightly less dangerous than matches. It's easy to create a sentence fragment (that's a bad thing) when you start a sentence with one of these critters:

Because Aardvark wanted to go fishing. (wrong)

When we get back from vacation. (wrong)

But once you're an adult, you're usually trusted with matches, and I believe you can also be trusted with subordinating conjunctions. As long as you include the main clause later in the sentence, words like *because, when,* and *unless* are acceptable sentence starters.

Because Aardvark wanted to go fishing, we had to get up at four in the morning.

When we get home from vacation, I'm going to buckle down at work.

The main clause comes after the comma and explains the subordinated part. Suddenly, it's not a sentence fragment; it's a complete sentence with a main clause and a dependent clause headed by a subordinating conjunction.

Truthfully, you can usually reverse the clause order to avoid starting the sentence with *because* and its friends, but you shouldn't have to. No grammatical rule exists to stand in your way.

We had to get up at four in the morning *because* Aardvark wanted to go fishing.

I'm going to buckle down at work *when* we get home from vacation.

Note that you don't need a comma between the two clauses when the dependent clause comes after the main clause. An exception to this rule is when the two parts of the sentence are in stark contrast. (Commas are often used to mark contrast when they would otherwise be left out.)

Squiggly was wide awake, *despite* getting up at four in the morning. (comma included because of contrast)

For more on subordinating conjunctions, see the appendix on page 197.

STARTING A SENTENCE WITH THE FANBOYS

Coordinating conjunctions are the FANBOYS of language.

F—For
A—And
N—Nor
B—But
O—Or
Y—Yet
S—So *(So can also be a subordinating conjunction)*

Typically, a coordinating conjunction joins other words, phrases, or clauses that have the same construction.

Squiggly was often distracted by this or that.

(This and that are both single nouns.)

Squiggly went to the store and bought some chocolate.

(Went to the store and bought some chocolate are both verb phrases.)

Squiggly went to the store, and Aardvark wondered when he would return.

(Squiggly went to the store and Aardvark wondered when he would return are both main clauses.)

But by now, you've probably figured out that I tend to be on the relaxed side of the language divide, and relaxed people think it's OK to start a sentence with a coordinating conjunction like *and, but,* and *or.* Actually, most sticklers think it's OK too. It's just a matter of style and formality. Starting a sentence with a coordinating conjunction is an informal style; it makes your writing sound conversational. In addition, a conjunction at the beginning usually draws attention to the sentence and adds punch.

I couldn't find the answer in my library. And I have a lot of books.

The punch is one of the reasons you don't want to overdo starting sentences with the FANBOYS in business writing—you don't want to sound punchy.

So, you might be thinking to yourself, "Why do I *think* I learned that it's wrong to start a sentence with a conjunction?" The answer is that many teachers cautioned students against starting sentences with conjunctions (especially in the past) because if you don't do it right, you can create sentence fragments. The risk is greater with subordinating conjunctions (see "Starting a Sentence with *Because*"), but the FANBOYS are sometimes considered guilty by association:

And looking for the answer. (wrong)

But hanging out at the beach. (wrong)

Also, I suspect that teachers believe kids are informal enough and don't need extra help from initial coordinating conjunctions to achieve an informal tone. How many things that you write in school call for an informal tone anyway? You don't often hear teachers saying, "Write an essay on the three branches of government by Monday, and make sure it has an informal tone."

The next question that always comes up is whether to follow the conjunction with a comma when you use it to start a sentence. A comma is not required after the conjunction unless there's an aside that would require commas anyway immediately after the conjunction.

And I love the holidays.

And, despite the extra work, I love the holidays.

STARTING A SENTENCE WITH *THERE ARE* AND *THERE IS*

Starting a sentence with *there are* and *there is* isn't grammatically incorrect, but the words are often unnecessary fluff:

There are many people who hate rain. (OK)

Many people hate rain. (better)

Also, starting a sentence with *there are* or *there is* can seem weak and boring. Usually, your sentence will be better with a stronger subject and verb. Which of the following sounds more exciting and helps you get a better visual image? (Hint: It's the one marked "better.")

There is a fly in my soup. (OK)

A fly is swimming laps in my soup. (better)

STARTING A SENTENCE WITH A NUMBER

Avoid starting a sentence with a number if you can, but if you have to contort your writing, just write out the number and get on with your work. Unless you enjoy torturing your readers, it's usually worth the effort to rewrite the sentence when you're working with long or complex numbers. Consider, in these examples, how much easier the second sentence is to read:

> **Twelve thousand eight hundred forty-two people attended the parade.**
>
> **The parade was attended by 12,842 people.**

The second sentence uses the passive voice (see chapter 8), but passive voice is better than writing out a humongous number and taking the risk that your readers' brains will be numb by the time they get to the verb.

When businesses report a lot of statistics and the natural place for the number is at the beginning of the sentence, they sometimes adopt a house style that puts the numeral in parentheses after the written-out number:

> **Seventy-two percent (72%) of respondents chose Hawaii as their preferred destination, 20% chose Alaska, and 8% chose Arizona.**

Some style guides say it is OK to start a sentence with a numeral when it is a year or a proper name (for example, the company name 3M), but more stringent style guides say to rewrite the sentence to avoid starting with a numeral. I think it is acceptable to start a sentence with a numeral in such cases, but use your own judgment—you know your audience better than I do.

> **1985 was a fabulous year. (questionable)**
>
> **3M hit their numbers this quarter. (questionable)**

IDIOT MANAGER ALERT

So now you can distinguish between the real rules and the myths about how to start a sentence. But knowing that myths are myths won't protect you from powerful people who don't have your level of language prowess.

Here's a list of what I like to call cover-letter grammar rules. They aren't real grammar rules, but I'd usually rather be hired than be right.

Don't start a sentence with

- *However*
- *Hopefully*
- A conjunction (*and, but, or,* etc.)
- *Because*
- A number

Getting started is often the hardest part of writing. Now that you know the rules, at least grammar confusion won't add to the stress of staring at a blank screen or piece of paper.

Chapter 4
PUNCH UP YOUR PUNCTUATION

YOU'VE BRUSHED UP ON YOUR grammar, you know how to choose the right words, and you've gotten over your writer's block by ignoring all the biddies who say you can't start a sentence with *however, and,* and the like. Now all you need is to string all those words together so they actually make sense. Punctuation helps with that.

Punctuation may seem like extraneous little hacks and splashes on the page, but those marks actually help readers stay on track. Punctuation is a polite gesture toward your reader: *Here, dear reader, allow me to guide you through this sentence. It's a long one, and it might be a little confusing, but I've provided clues and signposts along the way. I promise you won't get lost.*

We're going to start out easy with the period and work our way up to the more exotic punctuation marks like ellipses and asterisks. If we make it all the way to the interrobang, I might have to put on an evening gown!

PERIODICITY

The period is quite a straightforward punctuation mark. I think it's safe to say everyone knows that a period ends a sentence. What everyone doesn't know is how many spaces should come after a period and how to deal with periods in acronyms.

Space: The Final Frontier

If you learned to type on a typewriter, you were probably taught that you should leave two spaces after a period at the end of a sentence. The space bar on a typewriter makes a space that is the same size regardless of whether you are at the end of a word or the end of a sentence, which is the reason typewriter fonts are called monospaced fonts. In order to make a strong visual break between sentences on a typewriter, you need to type two spaces.

Now that most writing is done on computers, it is no longer necessary to type two spaces after a period at the end of a sentence. Word processing and typesetting software recognizes periods at the end of sentences, and if you are using a proportional font (which most fonts are these days), font designers have already made sure a properly sized space will be inserted between sentences.

Technically, whether you put one or two spaces after a period is still a matter of style. Some editors still prefer two spaces, but most style guides recommend one space, and page designers have written in begging me to advise people to leave only one space. They have told me that using two spaces can create unappealing rivers of white space throughout a document, and that if you are writing something that layout or design people will ever get their hands on, they will almost certainly have to go through your document and take out the extra space. So I recommend using only one space.

Acro-nymo-batics

No strict rule governs whether you should put periods after each letter in an acronym or initialism. Some publications put periods after each letter, arguing that because each letter is essentially an abbreviation for a word, periods are necessary. Other publications don't put periods after each letter, arguing that the copy looks cleaner without them and that because they are made up of all capital letters, the fact that they are abbreviations is implied.

When you have an abbreviation at the end of a sentence, don't use a second period. The period at the end of the abbreviation becomes a super period (not the technical term) that does the task of both shortening the abbreviation and ending the sentence. (If you think losing the clear

---

Abbreviation Information

Any shortened form of a word is an abbreviation, for example, *etc.* for *etcetera* and *Oct.* for *October*; but acronyms are special kinds of abbreviations, such as *ROFL* (*rolling on the floor laughing*) and *OPEC* (*Organization of Petroleum Exporting Countries*), that can be pronounced as words. This makes them a subset of abbreviations. All acronyms are abbreviations, but not all abbreviations are acronyms.

Initialisms are another type of abbreviation. They are often confused with acronyms because they are made up of letters, so they look similar, but they can't be pronounced as words. *FBI* and *CIA* are examples of initialisms because they're made up of the first letters of *Federal Bureau of Investigation* and *Central Intelligence Agency*, respectively, but they aren't usually pronounced as words. (People have written in to tell me that insiders often say "fibby" for *FBI*, but it's not something I've ever heard used among the general public.) *NASA*, on the other hand, is an acronym because even though it is also made up of the first letters of the department name (*National Aeronautics and Space Administration*), it is pronounced as a word, *NASA*, and not by spelling out the letters *N, A, S, A*.

ending to a sentence will confuse your readers, it's best to rewrite the sentence so the abbreviation doesn't come at the end, or write out the full word instead of using the abbreviation.) On the other hand, when you end a question or an exclamation with an abbreviation, you do include both the ending period of the abbreviation and the final question mark or exclamation point.

Squiggly always wanted to work for the F.B.I.

Doesn't Aardvark prefer the C.I.A.?

THE QUESTION MARK: HUH?

You think you already know how to ask questions, don't you? I wonder if you're right.

Everybody knows how to write a plain vanilla question: *what's new?* They're called direct questions. But there are trickier scenarios. What happens when a sentence seems to be half statement, half question? What if you're asking an indirect question, asking a question that also seems to require an exclamation point, dealing with a quotation that contains a question, and so on?

Questions Masquerading as Statements

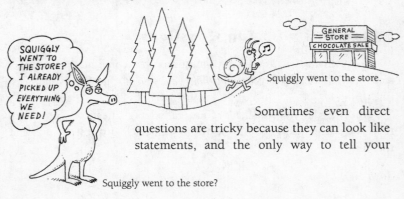

SQUIGGLY WENT TO THE STORE? I ALREADY PICKED UP EVERYTHING WE NEED!

GENERAL STORE
CHOCOLATE SALE

Squiggly went to the store.

Sometimes even direct questions are tricky because they can look like statements, and the only way to tell your

Squiggly went to the store?

reader otherwise is to add a question mark. There's a big difference in meaning between *Squiggly went to the store.* and *Squiggy went to the store?* Yet the only difference between the two sentences is that one ends with a period and one ends with a question mark. The question mark makes it a direct question that shows surprise. What the heck was he doing at the store?

A Question Flurry

What if you have a bunch of questions and you want to string them all together?

I love a scene in the movie *Cats & Dogs* where a dog realizes he can talk. It goes something like this: *You can hear me? Can I have a cookie? two cookies? four cookies? twenty cookies?* Those add-on questions at the end aren't complete sentences but they each get a question mark anyway. Since they aren't complete sentences, you usually don't capitalize the first letter, but the rules are vague. Some guides say to capitalize the first letter if the questions are nearly a sentence or have sentence-like status, so you have to use your own judgment. I don't consider *two cookies* to be nearly a sentence, but I may consider something like *two cookies and a squeaking ball to chase* to be nearly a sentence, which would make me consider capitalizing it.

Statements with Tag Questions

Now, what about those little questions that come at the end of a statement? *You didn't forget my birthday, did you? It's fun to play maracas, isn't it?*

Bits like *did you* and *isn't it* are called tag questions, and they turn the whole sentence into a question, so use a question mark at the end.

Indirect Questions

Do you have a curious nature? Do you wonder about things? When you wonder, your statements may sound like questions, but they're not direct questions, they're indirect questions, and they don't take a question mark. For example, *I wonder why he went to the store.* That's an indirect question—essentially a statement—so there's no question mark. *I wonder if Squiggly would lend me his maracas.* Again, it's not a question.

Indirect Questions Mixed with Direct Questions

It gets really crazy when you start mixing direct questions with other kinds of clauses. There are multiple ways to write something like *The question at hand is, who stole the cookies?* The simplest way to write that is to put a comma after the first clause and a question mark after the direct question.

Believe it or not, some style guides allow you to capitalize the first word in a direct question, even though it comes in the middle of a sentence: *The question at hand is, Who stole the cookies?* Supposedly, capitalizing the first word in the question places more emphasis on the question, but I think it makes the sentence look disjointed.

And if you think that looks weird, it gets even worse. If you flip the two parts around, you can put a question mark in the middle of your sentence: *Who stole the cookies? was the question at hand.*

It's good to know the rules, but these sentences seem so contorted that I believe it is better to try to rewrite them. I could easily convert the sentence to an indirect question: *Everyone wondered who stole the cookies.* Or I could use a colon to make the punctuation less odd: *One question remained: who stole the cookies?*

Surprising Questions

We made it to the interrobang! The fun begins, so imagine me in an evening gown. When you're asking a question in surprise such as *What?* it isn't appropriate to use multiple question marks or a question mark combined with an exclamation point. You're supposed to pick the terminal punctuation mark that is most appropriate, and use just one. Is your statement more of a question or more of an outburst?

I've always found that solution unsatisfactory, so I was thrilled to learn that there's an obscure punctuation mark that was designed exclusively for asking questions in a surprised manner. It's called an interrobang, and it looks like an exclamation point superimposed on a question mark.

You shouldn't use the interrobang in formal writing, but I would be delighted if people started using it on blogs and in other informal communications. If you have the Wingdings 2 or Palatino font in your word processing program, you can insert an interrobang as a special character.

SEMICOLONS: THE SENTENCE SPLICERS

Semicolons separate things. Most commonly, they separate two main clauses that are closely related to each other but could stand on their own as sentences if you wanted them to. I think of semicolons as sentence splicers: they splice sentences together.

> **It was below zero; Squiggly wondered if he would freeze to death.**

> **It was below zero. Squiggly wondered if he would freeze to death.**

One reason you may choose to use a semicolon instead of a period is if you wanted to add variety to your sentence structure; for example, if you thought you had too many short, choppy sentences in a row, you could add variety by using a semicolon to string together two main clauses into one longer sentence. But, when you use a semicolon, the main clauses should be closely related to each other. You wouldn't write, "It was below zero; Squiggly had pizza for dinner," because those two main clauses have nothing to do with each other. In fact, the other reason to use a semicolon instead of a period is to draw attention to the relationship between the two clauses.

Semicolons with Coordinating Conjunctions

An important thing to remember is that (with one exception) you never use semicolons with coordinating conjunctions such as *and, or,* and *but* when you're joining two main clauses. If you're joining two main clauses with a coordinating conjunction, use a comma: *It was below zero, and Squiggly wondered if he would freeze to death.*

The one exception is when you are writing a list of items and need commas to separate items within the list.

This week's winners are Herbie in Des Moines, Iowa; Matt in Irvine, California; and Jan in Seattle, Washington.

Because each item in the list requires a comma to separate the city from the state, you have to use a semicolon to separate the items themselves.

Semicolons with Conjunctive Adverbs

Finally, you use a semicolon when you use a conjunctive adverb to join two main clauses. Conjunctive adverbs are words such as *however, therefore,* and *indeed,* and they typically show some kind of relationship between the two main clauses. For a list of common conjunctive adverbs, see the appendix on page 196.

Aardvark is on vacation; therefore, Squiggly has to do extra work in this chapter.

Squiggly doesn't mind doing the extra work; however, he would like to be thanked.

Sometimes people find it hard to remember to use commas with coordinating conjunctions and semicolons with conjunctive adverbs, so if you can't keep the difference straight in your head, a quick and dirty tip is to remember that commas are smaller than semicolons and go with coordinating conjunctions, which are almost always short two- or three-letter words—small punctuation mark, small words. Semicolons are bigger and they go with conjunctive adverbs, which are almost always longer than three letters—bigger punctuation, bigger words.

The Colon: I Can't Wait to Read What Comes Next

One of my favorite language books, *Punctuate It Right,* has a wonderful name for the colon: the author calls it the mark of expectation or addition. That's because the colon signals that what comes next is directly related to the previous sentence.

Colons in Sentences

Colons can be used in a variety of situations, such as in titles, ratios, and writing out the time. But when you are using colons in sentences, the most important thing to remember is that colons are only used after statements that are complete sentences. Never use a colon after a sentence fragment. For example, it's correct to say that Squiggly has two favorite Thanksgiving dishes: stuffing and green-bean casserole. That's correct because *Squiggly has two favorite Thanksgiving dishes* is a complete sentence all by itself.

Notice how the items after the colon expand on or clarify what came before the colon. I referred to Squiggly's favorite dishes before the colon and then specifically named them after the colon. A quick and dirty tip for deciding whether a colon is acceptable is to test whether you can replace it with the word *namely*. For example, you could say *Squiggly has two favorite Thanksgiving dishes, namely, stuffing and green-bean casserole.* Most of the time, if you can replace a colon with the word *namely,* then the colon is the right choice. Nevertheless, there are also instances where you can use a colon and *namely* doesn't work. For example, *The band was wildly popular: they sold out the Colosseum.*

Going back to the complete sentence point, it would be wrong to say *Squiggly's favorite Thanksgiving dishes are: rolls and cranberry sauce* because *Squiggly's favorite Thanksgiving dishes are* is not a complete sentence by itself. You can often fix that problem by adding the words *the following* after your sentence fragment. For example, it would be fine to say *Squiggly's favorite Thanksgiving dishes are the following: stuffing and green-bean casserole* because you've made the thing before the colon a complete sentence by adding the words *the following.*

Colons in Lists

For some reason, people seem to get especially confused about how to use colons when they are introducing lists, but the good news is that the rules are the same whether you are writing lists or sentences: you use a colon when you could use the word *namely* and after something that could be a complete sentence on its own.

Squiggly has two favorite Thanksgiving dishes:

- **Stuffing**
- **Green-bean casserole**

Squiggly's two favorite Thanksgiving dishes are

- **Stuffing**
- **Green-bean casserole**

Colons in Salutations

Colons are also used after salutations in business letters.

Dear Mr. Smith:

Colons and Capitalization

Everyone always wants to know whether they should capitalize the first word after a colon. The answer is that it's a style issue, and it depends on what is following the colon. Although the most conservative grammarians would say that you should capitalize the first word after a colon when the colon introduces a complete sentence or more than one complete sentence, there are also grammarians who say capitalization isn't necessary. Since you never capitalize the first word after a colon if it is introducing something that isn't a complete sentence, I find it easier to adopt the less conservative lowercase rule for introducing complete sentences, and then all I have to remember is that the first word after a colon is always in lowercase (unless, of course, it is a proper name or something else that's always capitalized).

Colon Choices

People often ask me what the difference is between a semicolon and a colon. The first difference is that the purpose of a colon is to introduce or define something, and the purpose of a semicolon is to show that two clauses are related. Here's a clear example of a sentence that needs a colon.

- **Squiggly was fixated on something: chocolate.**

Here's a clear example of a sentence that needs a semicolon.

- **Squiggly was fixated; he couldn't get his mind off chocolate.**

The first sentence needs a colon because the second part (chocolate) is the definition of the first part (what Squiggly is fixated on). The second sentence needs a semicolon because the two parts are strongly related to each other. The second clause gives more of a description of what is going on in the first clause.

The second difference between a colon and a semicolon is that when you are joining things, you use a semicolon to join things of equal weight, whereas you can use a colon to join things of equal or unequal weight. For example, you can use either a semicolon or a colon to join two main clauses, but you can only use a colon to join a main clause with a lone noun. Here's an example: *Squiggly missed only one friend: Aardvark.* You couldn't use a semicolon in that sentence because the two parts are unequal.

One way that I remember the difference is to think of the different elements as railroad cars. (In my imagination it's the boxcars from the train in the *Schoolhouse Rock!* cartoon "Conjunction Junction.") I use a semicolon only if I'm joining two equal "boxcars." If I'm joining two unequal elements, such as a boxcar and a caboose, then I know I can't use a semicolon, and I consider whether a colon makes sense. So two equal sentence boxcars are joined by a semicolon, and unequal sentence boxcars and cabooses often get a colon (or a dash).

DASHES: I'M DASHING OFF TO BUY A GRAMMAR BOOK

The difference between a colon and a dash is subtle: they can both serve to introduce a related element after a sentence, but a dash is a stronger and more informal mark than a colon. Think of a colon as part of the sentence that just ambles along. *Squiggly has two favorite Thanksgiving dishes (and, now I'm going to tell you what they are): stuffing and green-bean casserole.* A colon informs readers that something more is coming along.

A dash, on the other hand—well, it's quite a dramatic thing. A dashing young man is certainly not an ordinary young man, and if you're dashing off to the store, you're not just going to the store, you're going in a flurry. A dash interrupts the flow of the sentence and tells the reader to get ready for an important or dramatic statement. If you added a dash to the "Thanksgiving" sentence it would conceptually read something like this: *Squiggly has two favorite Thanksgiving dishes (wait for it; wait for it)— stuffing and green-bean casserole. Wow!*

Given that there isn't anything exciting about Squiggly's favorite dishes, a dash may not be the best choice here, but it wouldn't be wrong. It would be a better choice if that sentence were part of a mystery novel where green-bean casserole was missing, and Squiggly was implicated as the thief. Then it could be a dramatic announcement that he loves green-bean casserole, and a dash would make more sense.

Making a Dash for It

Here's a very important rule about dashes: never, never, never use a hyphen in place of a dash. A hyphen is not a junior dash; it has its own completely separate use. Using a hyphen in place of a dash can cause your copy editor to have a mild fit.

There is no computer key for a dash; you need to insert a dash as a symbol. If for some reason you can't insert the dash symbol, for example if you are using a typewriter, use two hyphens right next to each other: --.

Dashes can also be used like commas or parentheses to set off part of a sentence. When you use dashes to set off a parenthetical element, you're using the strongest method possible to draw attention to it, so be sure it merits the drama.

THE HYPHEN: A NEVER-WERE-THERE-SO-FEW-SOLID-RULES PUNCTUATION MARK

You can use a hyphen to split a word at the end of a line, but you can also use a hyphen to join compound words.

A Dash of This, a Dash of That: Different Types of Dashes

You may have heard of two different kinds of dashes: em dashes (—) and en dashes (–). An em dash is longer than an en dash. Those may seem like strange names, but consider that historically the em dash was as long as the width of a capital typeset letter M, and the en dash was as long as the width of a capital typeset letter N. Now with computer typesetting, the widths of each may vary from font to font, with the width of an en dash always falling midway between a hyphen and an em dash.

The em dash is the kind of dash I was referring to in the main dash section; it is the kind of dash you use in a sentence. When people say, "Use a dash," they almost always mean the em dash.

The en dash is used much less frequently and usually only to indicate a range of inclusive numbers. You would use an en dash to write something like this:

- **Squiggly will be on vacation December 2 to December 9.**
- **Squiggly will be on vacation December 2–December 9.**

The *to* and the en dash between the dates indicate that Squiggly will not be in the office starting the second of December and will return on the tenth of December (because an en dash indicates that the numbers are inclusive of those two dates).

Whether you are using the longer em dash in a sentence or the shorter en dash to indicate an inclusive range, you can use your own judgment about whether to put spaces between the dash and the words around it—it's a style issue, so just be consistent.

The rules about when to hyphenate a compound word are a bit squidgy. Well, actually, they're a lot squidgy. The problem is that compound words go through an evolution from open compound (two separate words), to hyphenated compound, to closed compound (one word with the two parts shoved together)—and sometimes back again—and the changes can seem arbitrary. For example, when the *Shorter Oxford*

English Dictionary was released in 2007, it eliminated sixteen thousand hyphenated words. Some words (*leap-frog*) advanced to closed compound form (*leapfrog*), and other words (*pot-belly*) reverted back to open compound form (*pot belly*). The best advice I can give you is to pick a dictionary and consult it when you aren't sure whether to hyphenate a compound.

In very general terms, you use a hyphen to avoid confusion. For example, when two adjectives modify a noun, sometimes the sentence could be read two ways or be initially confusing to a reader, so you can use a hyphen to clarify which words go together:

Squiggly wanted a short haired dog.

(Could be read to mean that Squiggly wanted a short dog with hair.)

Squiggly wanted a short-haired dog.

(More clearly means that Squiggly wants a dog with short hair.)

Squiggly's short haired dog.   Aardvark's short-haired dog.

A hyphen also eliminates confusion when it is used to clarify pronunciation:

I need to re-press my jeans.

I need to repress those memories.

You often use a hyphen between two adjectives that come directly *before* the noun they modify, but not when they come *after* the noun they modify:

They are in a long-term relationship.

They are in it for the long term.

Despite the vast wiggle room in hyphen land, there are a few solid rules. You can confidently use a hyphen when you are joining a prefix to a word that must be capitalized, joining a letter to a word, and writing out numbers from twenty-one to ninety-nine:

- Anti-American
- Un-American
- Pre-Mesozoic

- X-ray
- A-list
- T-shirt

- Thirty-five
- Sixty-four
- Ninety-three

It's fine to occasionally make up an adjective using a long string of hyphenated words for effect, but don't overdo it to the point that you become an irritating hyphenate-for-no-reason writer.

Comma Comma Comma Comma
Comma Chameleon

Ah, the comma—the most versatile (and therefore confusing) punctuation mark in the English language. Many people were taught to use a
comma when they would naturally pause in a sentence, but that "rule" is
wrong. It's a decent way to guess if you have absolutely no idea whether
you need a comma, but it's not a rule and won't reliably lead you to the
right answer. It's "rules" like this that lead people to use commas like
confetti, throwing them around whenever the mood strikes them. Let
me get you started on your path to redemption.

Serial Comma

The comma people ask me about most often is the serial comma: the
comma that comes before the final conjunction in a list. Here's a sentence that uses a serial comma:

**Aardvark and Squiggly love chocolate, hiking, and
fishing.**

Whether to use the serial comma is a style issue, which is why so
many people are confused.

Although the British are less likely to use serial commas than Americans, primarily it's newspapers that allow writers to omit that final
comma. Newspapers are always looking to save space, and one argument for leaving out the comma is that it's unnecessary in simple sentences. Consider the same example without the serial comma:

**Aardvark and Squiggly love chocolate, hiking and
fishing.**

I didn't use a serial comma in that sentence, and there wasn't any
confusion. That's the main argument against using the serial comma: in
most cases leaving it out doesn't change anything.

Although the serial comma isn't always necessary, I favor it because often it does add clarity, and I believe in having a simple, consistent style instead of trying to decide whether you need something on a case-by-case basis. I also believe using the serial comma makes even simple lists easier to read. Really, unless space is incredibly expensive, I can't imagine why anyone would decide the best method is sometimes leave it out and sometimes add it in.

The one thing everyone does seem to agree on is that you have to use a serial comma when leaving it out would create confusion, as is often the case when the items in the list have internal conjunctions or are complex in some other way. Here's a sentence that could mean different things with and without the final comma because one of the list items has an internal conjunction: *Squiggly was proud of his new muffin recipes: blueberry, peanut butter and chocolate chip and coconut.*

Without a serial comma, you may not know whether the last recipe is coconut alone or a combination of chocolate chip and coconut. You can make the meaning clear in two ways: place the final comma after peanut butter or after chocolate chip, or rewrite the sentence so there is no ambiguity.

If you want to say that the final recipe is coconut alone, you can write *blueberry, peanut butter and chocolate chip, and coconut,* or if you in-sist on leaving out the serial comma, you can rewrite the list as *peanut butter and chocolate chip, blueberry and coconut.* But I still think the rewrite is more risky than the sentence with the serial comma because a reader who's just skimming the sentence could be tempted to think that coconut and blueberry is a combination.

Another case where leaving the comma out can be confusing is where the later items in the list can describe an earlier item. An oft-cited exam-ple is the made-up book dedication *To my parents, Ayn Rand and God.* A reasonable reader would assume there are four entities being thanked: Mom, Dad, Ayn Rand, and God; but without the serial comma you could also conclude that the two parents are Ayn Rand and God. A serial comma clears up any confusion: *To my parents, Ayn Rand, and God.*

Another oft-cited story involves a court case over an inheritance. If a will states that the fortune goes to Aardvark, Squiggly and Grammar

Girl, Aardvark can sue for—and win—50 percent (instead of 33.3 percent) of the inheritance because he can claim that Squiggly and Grammar Girl are a single unit. That would be a costly comma omission for Squiggly and Grammar Girl!

Finally, there are similar sentences where even a serial comma doesn't make the meaning clear. Consider this sentence: *I went to see Zack, an officer and a gentleman.*

Without the serial comma, *I went to see Zack, an officer and a gentleman* could mean that Zack is both an officer and a gentleman, or that I went to see three people: Zack, an unnamed officer, and an unnamed gentleman.

With the serial comma, *I went to see Zack, an officer, and a gentleman* could still mean two different things. It could mean I went to see three people (Zack, an unnamed officer, and an unnamed gentleman), or it could mean I went to see two people (Zack, who is an officer, and an unnamed gentleman).

So, the bottom line is that whether to use the serial comma is a style issue. Most publications except newspapers favor using it all the time, as do I, and all publications call for a serial comma when leaving it out could cause confusion. And sometimes sorting out your meaning is just too much for one little comma and the best option is to rewrite your sentence.

Adjective Commas

Commas and adjectives are another tricky area; fortunately, the rules are straightforward. If you can put the word *and* between the words, or if you can reverse the order of the adjectives and the sentence would still make sense, you can also use a comma.

Aardvark is a blue and small mammal.

Aardvark is a small and blue mammal.

Aardvark is a small, blue mammal.

(You can use and between the adjectives and reverse the order, so you use a comma.)

Sometimes it's a challenge to figure out whether a word that ends in *ly* is an adjective since adverbs also often end in *ly*. Remember that adjectives modify nouns and adverbs modify verbs (and things like other adverbs).

Aardvark took a long, daily run.

(Daily *is an adjective modifying the noun* run; *therefore, it is OK to use a comma.*)

Aardvark trains hard daily.

(Daily *is an adverb modifying the verb* trains; *therefore, don't use a comma. Note that you couldn't reverse the order of* hard *and* daily *in this sentence.*)

Aardvark is a friendly, blue beast.

(Friendly *is an adjective modifying the noun* beast; *therefore, it is OK to use a comma.*)

Aardvark is a fiercely loyal friend.

(Fiercely *is an adverb modifying the adjective* loyal; *therefore, don't use a comma. Note that you couldn't reverse the order of* fiercely *and* loyal *in this sentence.*)

Sentence-Joining Commas and Conjunctions

One of the most common ways to use commas is to separate two main clauses that are connected by a coordinating conjunction. That just means that when you join two things that could be sentences on their own with a word such as *and*, *but*, or *or*, you usually need a comma before the conjunction.

Squiggly ran to the forest, and Aardvark chased the peeves.

Squiggly ran to the forest could be a complete sentence, and *Aardvark chased the peeves* could be a complete sentence. To join them with a comma, you need the word *and* or some other coordinating conjunction.

In most cases, you need the noun in the second half of the sentence to use the comma. For example, the comma in the following sentence is wrong because there is no noun after it:

Squiggly ran to the forest, and chased the peeves. (wrong)

The only time you would use a comma in a sentence like the one above is if the second part of the sentence is in stark contrast to the first part of the sentence:

Squiggly cowered under a rock, but felt brave. (comma allowed because of contrast)

The Comma Splice

If you put a comma between two independent clauses without a conjunction (*Squiggly ran to the forest, Aardvark chased the peeves*) it's an error called a comma splice or a comma fault.

It's easy to see why the error is called a comma splice: the comma is used to splice together two complete sentences when that isn't the function of a comma.

The good news is that it's easy to fix a comma splice once you are aware of the problem. Because the two clauses are complete sentences, you can treat them that way and use a period where you had a comma. It's a period's job to separate complete sentences.

Squiggly ran to the forest. Aardvark chased the peeves.

If the two sentences are closely related to each other, for example, if Aardvark is chasing the peeves for the same reason Squiggly ran to the

The comma splice repair kit

forest, you can use a semicolon to connect the two sentences without a coordinating conjunction.

Squiggly ran to the forest; Aardvark chased the peeves.

If you imagine that there is a grammar toolbox, you can think of a semicolon as a "sentence splicer" because its job is to splice complete sentences together.

Commas aren't meant to join main clauses all by themselves; to force them into that role is to perpetrate a comma splice. That's bad, but it's easy to fix.

Run-on Sentences: Running on Empty

Run-on sentences are, in some ways, the opposite of comma splices: instead of using the wrong punctuation, they occur when you don't use any punctuation between two sentences. Many people mistakenly believe that run-on sentences are just long sentences, but run-on sentences are actually sentences that are smashed together without any punctuation. For that reason, they are also sometimes called fused sentences. Here's an example of a run-on sentence: *You're about halfway through this book you should be smarter by now.* Without internal punctuation, that is a run-on sentence. You can use the same tools we had in the comma splice repair kit to fix the fused sentence: periods, semicolons, dashes, colons, and coordinating conjunctions:

- **You're about halfway through this book. You should be smarter by now.**
- **You're about halfway through this book; you should be smarter by now.**
- **You're about halfway through this book, and you should be smarter by now.**
- **You're about halfway through this book—you should be smarter by now.***
- **You're about halfway through this book: you should be smarter by now.***

---

*A colon and dash aren't the best choices for this sentence (see the sections on colons and dashes on pages 92–96) but they can be used to repair some comma splices.

Commas Around Nonessential Elements

The August 2006 issue of *Wired* reported that there aren't any commas in Bart Kosko's book *Noise*. Apparently Kosko believes commas make you wait too long to get to the verb. He declared, "The comma is on the way out."

I disagree; but I think the people at Rogers Communications, Inc., in Canada, probably wish it were true. They recently lost $2.13 million in a court ruling that hinged on the placement of a comma in a contract. Yup, Grammar Girl was in heaven. Headline comma news!

The offending sentence reads like this: *The agreement shall continue in force for a period of five years from the date it is made, and thereafter for successive five year terms, unless and until terminated by one year prior notice in writing by either party.*

Rogers Communications thought that meant they had the deal locked up for the first five years and the other party could terminate any time after that with one year's notice, but the court ruled that grammar rules allowed the other party to terminate the contract at any time by giving one year notice, not just after the first five years. The reasoning was that "the comma placed before the phrase *unless and until terminated by one year prior notice in writing by either party* meant that the phrase qualified both the phrase *[the deal] shall be effective from the date it is made and shall continue in force for a period of five years from the date it is made* and the phrase *and thereafter for successive five year terms.*" In essence, they said the underlined part in the sentence was a parenthetical element. Somewhere in Canada, there were some very unhappy executives screaming at their lawyers about commas. (The ruling was eventually overturned on appeal based in part on disparities between the French and English versions of the contract, evidence of the history of negotiations, and "rules of punctuation and their application to contractual provisions.")

As the people at Rogers Communications surely learned, commas are used to separate parenthetical elements, asides, nonessential elements, and additional information from the rest of the sentence. In other words, commas offset something that could be left out but that wouldn't change the meaning of the rest of the sentence. Here are some additional examples:

The snail, which happened to be yellow, was named Squiggly.

His best friend, Squiggly, went to the store.

Commas and Conditional Sentences

Conditional sentences have an *if* clause such as *If you have any questions, let me know.* The action depends on something else. You will only let me know if you have questions. If you don't have questions, you won't let me know.

The rule is when the "if clause" is at the beginning of the sentence, you need a comma. But when the "if clause" is at the end of the sentence, you don't need a comma.

If you have any questions, let me know.

Let me know if you have any questions.

Commas with Interjections

Interjections at the beginnings of sentences are followed by commas (or exclamation points if you want to be more dramatic).

Indeed, he's quite irritating.

Yes! I do want to go to the beach.

Oh, he's coming along too?

Additional information about commas is also found in the sections "Tag Questions" and "Starting a Sentence with However."

ELLIPSES: MY THOUGHTS ARE TRAILING OFF . . .

The Omission Ellipsis

The most common and formal use of ellipses is to indicate an omission. If you're quoting someone and you want to shorten the quote, you use ellipses to show where you've dropped words or sentences.

Here's a quote from the book *Our Mutual Friend* by Charles Dickens: "I cannot help it; reason has nothing to do with it; I love her against reason."

Now far be it from me to edit Dickens, but if I were a journalist under a tight word limit looking at that quote, I'd be tempted to shorten it to this: "I cannot help it . . . I love her against reason." That middle part—*reason has nothing to do with it*—seems redundant, and taking it out doesn't change the meaning. Dot-dot-dot and it's gone, which saves me seven words. Clearly, literature and journalism are not the same thing.

Integrity is essential when using ellipses in this way. It's fine to use an ellipsis to tighten up a long quote by omitting unnecessary words, but it's important that you don't change the meaning. It's wrong to omit words to misrepresent what someone has said. For example, imagine what an unethical writer could do with the following quote:

> **"*Gigli* was the best movie of 2003—if you were a vapid tabloid groupie who couldn't get enough of Ben Affleck and Jennifer Lopez."**

It would be easy to use ellipses and omissions to make the quote sound as if the writer loved *Gigli*. Here's the revised quote:

> **"*Gigli* was the best movie of 2003. . . ."**

See? Chop off the qualifier at the end, and you've got a completely different quote. Of course, that is an obvious and egregious example; you would never do that, but be careful not to introduce more subtle changes in meaning when you use ellipses (and when you are editing quotes in general).

The E-mail Ellipsis

Now, on to the other use of ellipses—the use you frequently see in e-mail messages, where the ellipsis is used to indicate a pause or a break in the writer's train of thought. I read a lot of complaints in e-mail groups and a lot of speculation about what these ellipses mean. However, speculation isn't necessary because ellipses can be used for the following reasons to indicate a pause or falter in dialogue: to show that

- Time has passed
- A list is unfinished
- A speaker has trailed off in the middle of a sentence or left something unsaid

So it is allowable to use ellipses to indicate pauses or breaks in the writer's train of thought, as you see so frequently done in e-mail, especially where a break is meant to feel uncertain. Nevertheless (and this is a BIG nevertheless), most people who use ellipses in e-mail overdo it—a lot.

You should not replace all normal punctuation with ellipses. You should not allow the sweet lure of ellipses to muddle your ability to write a complete sentence. Use ellipses in these ways if you must, but

Three-Dot Journalism

A couple of famous newspaper writers have used ellipses instead of periods to separate their rambling thoughts. Larry King heartily used ellipses in his *USA Today* column, as did Herb Caen in his *San Francisco Chronicle* column. In fact, Herb Caen is reported to have coined the phrase *three-dot journalism* to describe such writing, and he was so beloved in San Francisco that when he died the city named a street after him—and included an ellipsis in the name: Herb Caen Way. . . .

use them sparingly, and know that although it's grammatically correct, it's considered by some to be annoying and cheap.

Formatting Ellipses

So, now that you know how to use ellipses, you need to know how to make them. An ellipsis consists of exactly three dots called ellipsis points—never two dots, never four dots—just three dots.

Most style guides call for a space between the dots. Typesetters and page designers use something called a thin space or a nonbreaking space that prevents the ellipsis points from getting spread over two lines in a document. Also, many fonts have an ellipsis symbol that you can insert, but for everyday purposes, it's fine to use regular spaces between the ellipsis points. Type period-space-period-space-period. Just make sure your ellipsis doesn't get broken up and spread out over two lines.

Also, there should always be a space on each side of an ellipsis. The ellipsis is usually standing in for a word or sentence, so just imagine that it's a word itself, and then it's easy to remember to put a space on each side.

If you're omitting something that comes after a complete sentence, meaning that your ellipsis has to follow a period, put the period at the end of the sentence just as you normally would, type a space, and then type or insert your ellipsis. Again, you're treating the ellipsis as if it were a word. This will result in four dots in a row with spaces between each dot, but this is not a four-dot ellipsis—there's no such thing. It is a period followed by a regular three-dot ellipsis.

Oddly, you don't treat an ellipsis as a word if it comes at the end of a sentence that requires terminal punctuation like a period, question mark, or exclamation point. In that case you still put a space on each side of the ellipsis. For example, if your original sentence is *Aardvark is coming home on Thursday!* and you wanted to make it shorter, you would write it like this: *Aardvark is coming home . . . !*

Fortunately, most style guides don't call for an ellipsis when you omit something at the end of a quote, so you don't have to deal with it too often. (Putting an ellipsis at the beginning of a quote is also usually not necessary, but again it is a matter of style.)

THE ASTERISK: A RISKY PROPOSITION

Who would have thought a simple punctuation mark could cause a stir? But sports is a nutty business—people actually get paid to play games—so why be surprised that sports fans get all atwitter about asterisks?

The asterisk of the moment waits for Barry Bonds. When he broke the record for career home runs, people started talking about putting an asterisk next to his name in the record book because of the steroid controversy surrounding his career. I couldn't care less about the baseball record, but I was thrilled about the emergence of another punctuation-related news story!

The asterisk is that little star above the number 8 key on your keyboard, and the word *asterisk* actually comes from the Latin and Greek words for "little star." *Asterisk* can also be used as a verb to mean that you've marked something with the little star; for example, *Some sportswriters want the baseball commissioner to asterisk Barry Bonds' record.*

It's pronounced "aste-risk." It's common to hear people call it an "aste-rick" or "aste-rix," but the correct pronunciation is "aste-risk."

Asterexasperation

My first rule for using an asterisk is to always make sure it refers to something at the bottom of the page. It makes me crazy when ads have an asterisk next to some offer, and then you can't find what it means. More than once I've seen something such as *Jackhammers, 20% off,** and then nothing else on the page to indicate what the asterisk means. Does it mean I get 20 percent off only if it is a Sunday and my name is Squiggly? I hate that! Two Grammar Girl podcast listeners suggested new words to go with these aggravating asterisks: Scott T. calls it an "exasperisk," and Chuck Tomasi refers to the feeling upon seeing one as "asterexasperation."

Star Power: How to Use an Asterisk

Today, you place an asterisk after something you want to comment on or qualify. Historically, asterisks were also used to show that something was omitted or that there was a passage of time, but that use has been largely taken over by the ellipsis. Today, the asterisk is for commenting, especially when you need to avoid letters or numbers, such as when adding comments to mathematical or chemical equations. Using symbols will prevent people from confusing your comment marks as part of the equations. You wouldn't want readers thinking your second comment note means to square the equation!

Symbols: When an Asterisk Is the First of Many

If you have to include both citations and long comments in a document, you should use symbols for the footnoted comments—and the order matters! Start with the asterisk and then continue with the dagger, double dagger, section mark, parallels, and number sign. If you need more symbols, you start over in the sequence and double each symbol: double asterisk, double dagger, double double dagger, etcetera. The specific symbols that are used for citations, and their order, vary from publication to publication, so you should always check the style guide or instructions to authors.

* † ‡ § ‖ #

Asterisks are also used to replace letters in obscene words to avoid offense—*h*ll*, *sh*t*, and *d*mn*, for example.

When you combine an asterisk with other punctuation marks, the asterisk goes after every punctuation mark except the dash.

There is a controversy about Barry Bonds' home run record*—whether to include an asterisk.

The Barry Bonds home run record,* broken in San Francisco, may be marked with an asterisk in the record books.

San Franciscans celebrated Barry Bonds' home run record.*

Negative Connotations

I have a theory that when used alone, an asterisk has a more negative connotation than a number or a letter. Think about advertisements: the asterisk always indicates a limitation on what seems like a great offer. Also, when linguists want to show examples of incorrect words or sentences, they often mark them with an asterisk. And finally, thinking back to Barry Bonds, I'm sure the proposed asterisk next to his name in the record book isn't something he's looking forward to seeing.

The Nathan Hale

Among computer programmers, the asterisk is sometimes called a "Nathan Hale." The name comes from a reimagining of the famous quote Hale made before being hanged—*I only regret that I have but one life to lose for my country*—to *I only regret that I have but one asterisk (ass to risk) for my country.*

Had Hale actually uttered "ass to risk" instead of "life to lose," this kind of mishearing (*ass to risk → asterisk*) would be classified as a slip of the ears called a Mondegreen.

---

*The record Bonds broke in 2007 was for the most home runs hit in a career.

FORMATTING VERTICAL LISTS

Experts have raised valid concerns that people overuse lists in Power-Point presentations and for presenting complex information, but the scant attention to lists in most style guides has always baffled me because you can hardly open a Web page, marketing brochure, or user manual without walking smack into a list. Marketing experts and Web designers know that most people visually scan such simple or instructional documents instead of reading every word and that lists improve a scanner's ability to remember key points.

Bullets, Numbers, and Letters

If you're going to use a list, the first question to ask yourself is what kind of list you should use.

Bullets are just big dots, and you use them to make a bulleted list when the order of the items doesn't matter. For example, you could use bullets to list the items you want everyone to bring to a beach party:

I wish I were in Santa Cruz right now. I'd have a party and make s'mores. Everyone would need
- Chocolate bars
- Graham crackers
- Marshmallows
- Pointy sticks

When the order isn't important, I usually list the items alphabetically or in some other way that seems to make sense. The list in the s'mores example is alphabetical, but if I called the pointy sticks something that didn't fall at the end alphabetically, I still would have grouped all the food items together and put sticks at the end. In marketing materials, you probably want to put your most important product feature or selling point first.

Numbers are reserved for instances where the items in the list need to follow a specific sequence. You could use numbers to list the stepwise tasks that are required in order to start up a piece of machinery. For example.

> **When I turn on my laptop, I**
> 1. Open the cover
> 2. Push the start button
> 3. Make tea while the applications load

Letters are useful when you're implying that readers need to choose individual items or when items don't need to follow a specific sequence, but you want to refer back to an item later.

> **Visit the Grammar Girl website (http://grammar**
> **.quickanddirtytips.com) for free extras:**
> a. Goofy grammar photos
> b. Quizzes
> c. An e-mail newsletter

Letters make sense with that list because the order doesn't matter, and I can refer to item (b) if I want to promote the free quizzes again later. You can use capital or lowercase letters for your list. It seems to be more common to use lowercase letters, but just make sure you are consistent.

Remember from the section about colons that if your lead-in statement is a complete sentence, then you use a colon at the end to introduce your list. On the other hand, if your lead-in statement is a sentence fragment, don't use a colon.

Capitalization

After you've completed the introductory sentence, your next question will be whether to capitalize the first letter in the statements that come after your bullets, numbers, or letters.

If your list item is a complete sentence, capitalize the first letter. If your list item isn't a complete sentence, you can choose whether to capitalize the first letter—it's a style issue. The only thing that is important is to be consistent. I capitalize the first letter of everything in lists because it's easier to remember to capitalize everything than it is to remember to capitalize complete sentences and use lowercase for sentence fragments.

Punctuation

With capitalization covered, you're on to your items, and at the end of the first one you have to decide what kind of punctuation to use.

If your list items are complete sentences, or if at least one list item is a fragment that is immediately followed by a complete sentence, use normal terminal punctuation: a period, question mark, or exclamation point.

For the following reasons, I feel bad for people who don't visit the website:
- They miss the goofy grammar photos.
- They can't take the free quizzes.
- They can't sign up for the e-mail newsletter that includes free grammar tips.

If your list items are single words or sentence fragments, you can choose whether to use terminal punctuation. Again, the important thing is to be consistent. I don't use terminal punctuation after single words or sentence fragments. I think periods look strange after things that aren't sentences.

The following additional content is available on the website:
- Goofy grammar photos
- Free quizzes
- A free e-mail newsletter

Finally, your text will be easier to read if you don't put commas or semicolons after the items, and don't put a conjunction such as *and* before the last item. They are unnecessary clutter.

Parallelism

OK, now that you've got the mechanics down for lists, don't forget to be a good writer and make sure all of your list items are parallel. That means each list item should be structured the same way. They should all be fragments or they should all be complete sentences. If you start one bullet point with a verb, start every bullet point with a verb. Here's an example of a list that uses parallel construction:

For Aardvark, a vacation involves
- Attending lectures
- Reading books
- Seeing sights

Each bullet point is formed the same way—each one starts with a verb.

On the other hand, even though the following list is grammatically correct, it's considered poor writing because the list items aren't parallel.

For Aardvark, a vacation involves
- Attending lectures
- Books
- Many trips to famous destinations

Style

Many of the points I've covered in this section are style issues, meaning that I've run across multiple books and online style guides that make different recommendations. My recommendations are based on my assessment after checking about twenty different grammar handbooks and style guides and on what seems logical to me. For example, I didn't find any source that discussed how to order items in a bulleted list, so I made up the recommendation to write them alphabetically because it seems to be the best solution. However, if your organization has a designated style guide, be sure to check it to see if your house style differs from any of my recommendations.

QUOTATION MARKS: YOU CAN QUOTE ME

Yeah, He Actually Said That

The most common use of double quotation marks is to surround direct quotations or spoken words. Something inside quotation marks is assumed to be *exactly* what the person being quoted said or wrote; so if you make changes, you must indicate them with ellipses (also see the section on ellipses), brackets, or the abbreviation *sic* in square brackets (which is Latin for "thus; so" and indicates the error was made by the speaker or original writer and not by the current writer).

> **In his bulletin, Smith wrote, "Pork bellys rose eighty, and I mean percent not dollars, last year." (original quotation)**

> **In his bulletin, Smith wrote, "Pork bellys [*sic*] rose eighty [percent] . . . last year." (edited quotation)**

> **According to Smith's bulletin, pork bellies rose eighty percent last year. (paraphrased quotation)**

Typically, if you have to make too many changes to a quotation, it is better to paraphrase the statement.

Quotation Confusion

It's common to hear people use the verb *quote* as a shortened form of quotation, as in "I filled my notebook with *quotes* from *The Daily Show*," but such use is technically wrong. It should be, "I filled my notebook with *quotations* from *The Daily Show*." Now, I agree the correct way sounds kind of pretentious, and given that a lot of reference sources have extra entries discussing how the misuse is widespread, you aren't going to sound illiterate if you use *quote* incorrectly, but it is still good to know the difference and stick to *quotation* in formal writing.

Let's Get Snarky

Double quotation marks can also be used to indicate that a word is special in some way. I bet you've all seen quotation marks used as something called "scare quotes," which are quotation marks put around a word to show that the writer doesn't buy into the meaning. For example, I could write the sentence *Women achieved "equality" when they were granted the right to vote in 1920.* The quotation marks would indicate that although women getting the right to vote was heralded as equality at the time, I don't think it was enough of a gain to merit the word *equality*. More often, though, scare quotes (which are also sometimes called sneer quotes) are used to impart a sense of irony or disdain. They're especially common in nasty political commentary, as in *Politicians "care" about their constituents.*

Mixed Company

Commas and Periods

One reason you are probably confused about mixing quotation marks with other punctuation marks is that American English and

British English have different rules about quotation marks. So if you read the BBC and *The New York Times* websites on the same day, you'll see punctuation done two different ways.

In the United States, periods and commas go inside the quotation mark. In Britain, they go outside the quotation mark.

Squiggly said, "No." (United States)

Squiggly said, "No". (Britain)

"No," said Squiggly. (United States)

"No", said Squiggly. (Britain)

Question Marks and Exclamation Points

Where do you put the question mark or exclamation point when you're using quotation marks? It depends on the sentence—is the whole thing a big question or exclamation, or is only the part in quotation marks a question or exclamation?

Using question marks as an example, if the whole sentence is a question, then you put the question mark outside the quotation mark.

What do you think Squiggly meant when he said, "The fish swam darkly up the river"?

The whole sentence is a question, so the question mark goes at the very end (outside the quotation mark).

On the other hand, if only the quotation is a question, then the question mark goes inside the quotation mark.

Squiggly ran up to Aardvark and asked, "Where are the fish?"

The question mark goes inside the quotation mark because the only part of the sentence that is a question is *Where are the fish?* (You don't need a period after the quotation mark. Despite being inside the quotation mark, the question mark serves as the terminal punctuation.) It works the same way with exclamation points.

It helps to remember that the question mark (or exclamation point) stays attached to the question (or exclamation)—whether it makes up the whole sentence or just the quotation.

The Single Life

Single quotation marks are like backup double quotation marks— you pull them out of your bag of tricks when you've already used double quotation marks. The most common use is when you are quoting someone who is quoting someone else. You enclose the primary speaker's comments in double quotation marks, and then you enclose the thing they are quoting in single quotation marks. For example, imagine you've interviewed Aardvark for a magazine article about his harrowing ordeal with the arrow.

> **Aardvark said, "Squiggly yelled, 'Watch out,' as the arrow was coming toward me."**

If you're ever in the extremely rare position of having to nest another quote inside a sentence like that, you would use double quotation marks again for the quote inside of the single quotation marks.

> **Aardvark said, "Squiggly yelled, '*Sir Fragalot says,* "*Watch out,*" ' as the arrow was coming toward me."**

Note that there are three levels of quotations in that last example sentence: the part in bold, the part in bold italics, and the part in underlined bold italics.

Single quotation marks are also sometimes used when there's a quote in a headline, and they are used to highlight words with special meaning in certain disciplines such as philosophy, theology, and linguistics.

Suspensive Hyphens: Leave Me Hanging

You may not have known they were called suspensive hyphens, but you know you've seen those hyphens that seem to be hanging in the air. They most often occur with numbers:

Do you want a one- or two-bedroom apartment?

Please pick up a ten- to twelve-foot pipe at the hardware store.

Suspensive hyphens are economical—there's no need to name the second part of the compound when you're going to get to it in a second. Be patient; it will show up soon.

EXCLAMATION POINT

The exclamation point adds emphasis and indicates a strong emotion—surprise, panic, urgency, etc. Don't overuse it! (See page 68 for a discussion about exclamatory sentences and page 121 for a discussion about mixing an exclamation point with quotation marks.)

PARENTHESES

Asides

Parentheses are beautiful; I think of them as bookends for fun little statements. The words inside of parentheses are called parenthetical elements, and they often act as asides. They are things you don't need to say, but want to say anyway. They can clarify, direct, or give a sense of the writer's frame of mind.

Everyone loved Sigler's new book (*Ancestor*).

Also see the section on commas (pp. 100–8) and dashes (pp. 95–96).

I'm fantasizing (just fantasizing, mind you) about skipping town and taking a job as a juggler.

Parentheses with Other Punctuation Marks

If the parenthetical element is a complete sentence, the terminal punctuation goes inside the parenthesis. If the parenthetical element is not a complete sentence, but comes at the end of a sentence, the terminal punctuation goes outside the parenthesis.

Squiggly had many allergy symptoms. (He was itching, sneezing, and coughing.)

Squiggly had many allergy symptoms (itching, sneezing, and coughing).

If you have a complete sentence inside parentheses, and it falls inside another complete sentence, you don't capitalize the first letter of the parenthetical sentence and you don't use terminal punctuation unless the sentence requires a question mark or exclamation point.

Squiggly loves (we mean he truly adores) fish.

Squiggly loves (should we say adores?) fish.

APOSTROPHES

I saved apostrophes for the end of the chapter because they are, hands down, the most troublesome punctuation mark. My listeners often send me photos of objects (T-shirts, signs, packaging, etc.) that contain grammar mistakes, and about 90 percent of those photos are of

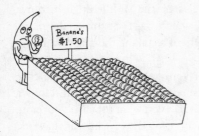 

signs that misuse apostrophes. Apostrophe errors are so common on produce signs that an apostrophe that is misused in a sign like "Banana's $1.50" actually has a name: the greengrocer's apostrophe.

Apostrophes have two main uses in the English language: they stand in for something that's missing, and they can be used to make a word possessive.

Apostrophes first showed up in the 1500s as a way to indicate omissions. Today, the most common place to find this kind of apostrophe is in contractions such as *can't* (for *cannot*), *that's* (for *that is*), and *it's* (for *it is* or *it has*). But apostrophes can also be used in fun ways. If you're writing fiction, you can replace letters with apostrophes to reflect a character's dialect; for example, you could write, "I saw *'em* talkin' yonder," to indicate that the speaker said *'em* instead of *them* and *talkin'* instead of *talking.*

It's no wonder that people are confused about apostrophes because new uses were introduced in the 1600s and again in the 1700s, and it wasn't until the mid-1800s that people even tried to set down firm rules. One major new use for the apostrophe was to indicate possession. For example, *Aardvark's pencil,* where there is an apostrophe s at the end of *Aardvark,* means that the pencil belongs to Aardvark. It does not mean the plural of *Aardvark,* and it does not mean "The aardvark is pencil."

An interesting side note is that it doesn't seem so strange that an apostrophe s is used to make words possessive once you realize that in Middle English it was common to make words possessive by adding *es* to the end. For example, the possessive of *ston* (the Middle English equivalent of *stone*) would have been *stones,* which was the same as the plural. So today, the apostrophe can be thought of as taking the place of the *e* in the possessive case of long ago.

The bottom line is that whenever you are using apostrophes, especially if you are making signs or flyers, take a second and a third look at them to make sure you're doing it right. Do you want to make your noun possessive, are you making a contraction, or do you instead have the plural form of a noun that shouldn't include an apostrophe?

Singular Words That End with S

Many people are surprised to learn that there are two ways to make words that end with s possessive. It's true, and there are even justices in the U.S. Supreme Court who have squabbled about how to do it: is it *Kansas's statute,* with an apostrophe s, or *Kansas' statute,* with just an apostrophe at the end? Justice Clarence Thomas wrote the majority opinion for *Kansas v. Marsh* and prefers to leave off the extra s, referring to *Kansas' statute* (with just an apostrophe at the end), whereas Justice David Souter wrote the dissenting opinion and prefers the double s of *Kansas's statute* (with an apostrophe before the final s).

So who's right? Neither. Both. Justice Thomas' name ends with an s, so you might guess that he is more invested in the topic, but style books make different recommendations, some suggesting you should leave off the extra s, and others recommending that you add the apostrophe s to almost all singular words that end with s. (The exceptions are words such as *Moses* and *Bridges* that end with an s that makes an "iz" sound, and classical names such as *Zeus* and *Venus,* and *Jesus.* Some style guides suggest that all these words should end with just an apostrophe (e.g., *Moses' tablets*). So our first tough issue—how to make words that end with s possessive—doesn't actually have an answer; it's a style issue and you can do it either way. Many people have written in telling me the rule they use is that if they pronounce the second s, they write it out; and if not, they leave it off. Nevertheless, I prefer to pick one style and stick with it—I leave off the final *s* because doing so looks cleaner and saves space.

Plural Words That End with *S*

I always feel bad when the answer is that there isn't an answer, as in the previous section, so here's an easier situation that has a firm rule: if the word ending with *s* is plural, such as *peeves,* then you just add an apostrophe at the end to make it possessive. For example, you could write, "The peeves' escape route was blocked" to indicate that a group of peeves needed to find another way out of danger.

Plural words that don't end with *s,* such as *children,* do take an apostrophe *s* at the end for possession. For example, you could write, "Fortunately, the children's room had a hidden doorway" and "We sell children's books."

The Plural of a Single Letter

Here's a tricky issue with a definite answer: how do you make a single letter plural, as in *Mind your* p*'s and* q*'s*? It's shocking, but you actually use an apostrophe before the *s*! It looks possessive, but it isn't. The apostrophe is there just to make it clear that you're writing about multiple *p*'s and *q*'s. The apostrophe is especially important when you are writing about *a*'s, *i*'s, and *u*'s because without the apostrophe readers could easily think you are writing the words *as, is,* and *us.*

Making Abbreviations Plural

Making abbreviations plural used to be more of a gray area, but I'm thrilled to report that the last prominent holdout I'm aware of (*The New York Times*) recently stopped using apostrophes to make abbreviations plural. The *NYT* used to write about *CD's* when they meant multiple CDs. But they don't do it anymore, and I finally feel as if I can firmly recommend against using apostrophes to make abbreviations plural!

Compound Possession

If you're trying to write about possession and have two subjects, you have to decide if the two people possess something together or separately. Here's an example: *Squiggly and Aardvark's religious beliefs*. The rule is if the two people share something, you use one apostrophe *s*. So if Squiggly and Aardvark have the same religious beliefs, it is correct to say *Squiggly and Aardvark's beliefs* (with only one apostrophe *s* after the last noun). On the other hand, if Squiggly and Aardvark have different beliefs, then you would say *Squiggly's and Aardvark's beliefs*.

The rule is if they each possess something different, then you use two apostrophe *s*'s. The quick and dirty tip for remembering the rule is to think about luggage and hair dryers. Imagine that two women are going on the same trip; if they are sharing an adventure, they can share a hair dryer on the trip, so then they can share the apostrophe *s* too (*Gail and Mignon's adventure*); but if they are each going on their own separate adventure, then they each need their own hair dryer, and they each need their own apostrophe *s* (*Gail's and Mignon's adventures*). So an apostrophe *s* is like a hair dryer: you don't need to bring two if you are going to stay in the same hotel room. When one of the words is a pronoun, you use the possessive pronoun: *Squiggly's and my tree is thriving*. (As a rule of politeness, put yourself last in a list of people.)

Greeting Card Grammar

As you learned in the section "Words That End with *S*," you could go to Bob Jones' house or Bob Jones's house—both are correct. But what if you have a family? Bob, Amy, and their children are the Joneses. The possessive form of *Joneses* is *Joneses'*. If the Joneses invite people over for dinner, their invitation could read two different ways:

- **Please come to the Joneses' house for dinner. (possessive)**
- **The Joneses invite you to dinner. (plural)**

Chapter 5
BIG AND TALL:
CAPITALIZATION

I TOOK GERMAN IN HIGH SCHOOL, and one of the first things I noticed was that all the nouns were capitalized. Common nouns and proper nouns—they all get capitalized in German. English is different, but there was a period between roughly 1600 and 1800 when it was trendy to capitalize all the nouns in English too. Next time you're browsing the U.S. Constitution with friends, you can impress them by pointing out that all the nouns are capitalized because the document was written during this trendy capitalize-all-nouns period.

PRIM AND PROPER: PROPER NOUNS

If you remember the Saturday morning cartoon *Schoolhouse Rock!,* you'll remember that a noun is a person, place, or thing. ("Things" can

A proper noun is capitalized and names a specific person, place, or thing.

be concrete things like rocks or abstract things like courage.) But for capitalization purposes, English nouns are divided into two types: proper nouns and common nouns.

The difference is that proper nouns name *specific* people, places, or things and common nouns name *general* people, places, or things. Proper nouns like *Squiggly, Mississippi River,* and *Golden Gate Bridge* are capitalized because they are proper nouns that name specific people, places, or things—they are names. On the other hand, *snail, river,* and *bridge* aren't capitalized because they are common nouns that don't refer to any one individual person, place, or thing.

Adjectives that are derived from proper nouns are capitalized too. For example, if Aardvark lives in Seattle, he is a Seattleite.

So names are easy, they are capitalized, but some words are less clear, and then you have to decide if they are naming something specific or something general. (And even then, sometimes the answer isn't clear and you just have to use your best judgment.) Here are two examples:

Ground Zero

Last year, I realized that sometimes I see the words *ground zero* capitalized and sometimes I don't. Back in 2001, it seemed as if the name

Ground Zero got assigned to the site of the World Trade Center in New York almost immediately. Traditionally, *ground zero* means the site of a nuclear explosion, and sometimes it is used to refer to the site of a more general explosion or an area where rapid change has taken place. In those general instances, *ground zero* would be a common noun and wouldn't be capitalized. On the other hand, although there are a few dissenters, most notably *The New York Times,* most people agree that *Ground Zero* is the name of the specific site of the former World Trade Center; therefore, it's a proper noun that needs to be capitalized when it is used in that way.

Depression

Depression is another word that's sort of like *ground zero,* in that sometimes it's a proper noun and sometimes it's a common noun. If you're talking about a general economic depression, then it's lowercased; but if you're talking about the Great Depression, then you are referring to a specific historical period, so it's capitalized.

Planets

Have you ever heard that people can be irrational about their home? Well, since earth is our home, maybe that explains why it doesn't follow the typical capitalization rules.

All the other planet names (*Mars, Jupiter,* etc.) are always capitalized because they're names that refer to specific places, but for some reason, most people treat *earth* differently and don't capitalize it. (When you are using the word *earth* to refer to dirt, of course it's lowercased.) Sometimes you'll see *earth* capitalized when it's listed with all the other planet names or when it's referred to in an astronomical way. For example, it will likely be capitalized in a sentence talking about space travel like, "We plan to leave Earth in January and arrive at Mars in October," but it is likely to be lowercased in a sentence where it is used more generically, like, "I'm wishing for peace on earth and goodwill to men." So the word *earth* is an exception to the rule that something is always a proper noun and capitalized if it names one specific place. I hate exceptions, but it's good to know about them.

TALK GRAMMAR TO ME, BABY

A quick and dirty tip is that nicknames are capitalized, and terms of endearment are not. So to take a line from *Dirty Dancing*, "Nobody puts Baby in a corner." But *baby* would not be capitalized in a more generic setting: *Come here, baby.*

A similar rule holds true for family names such as *mother, mom, father,* and *dad. Mom* is generally a capitalized nickname, whereas *mother* is generally a lowercased generic term:

> **How's your *mother* these days?**
>
> **How's *Mom* these days?**

Aunt, uncle, and *cousin* are also usually lowercased unless they are part of someone's name:

> **Did you call *Aunt Mathilda*?**
>
> ***My aunt Mathilda* always hiccoughs during dinner.**

THE ENGLISH DEPARTMENT AT HILL AND DALE COLLEGE: DEGREES AND DEPARTMENTS

People often think there is a typo on my "About Grammar Girl" Web page because it says I have an undergraduate degree in English (capitalized) and a graduate degree in biology (lowercased).

Although I've never claimed to be perfect, that isn't a typo. *English* is capitalized because it is derived from a proper noun (*England*), and *biology* is lowercased because it is not derived from a proper noun. Similarly,

Spanish, Italian, and *German* are capitalized and *chemistry, math,* and *visual arts* are not.

"Department" is capitalized when it is part of the exact name of a specific department, but not when it is used generically as a common noun:

> **The *Department of Computer Gaming* issued an announcement.**
>
> **The *department* chairperson just won the World of Warcraft pumpkin-carving contest.**

THIS TITLE USES TITLE CAPS

When you're writing a title, you are confronted with a shocking number of formatting options. How you decide to handle capitalization is up to you: it's a style issue! If your boss, editor, or teacher has a preferred style, you should use that; but if you're the master of your own universe (e.g., you're writing on your own blog), you're free to choose any of the following methods:

> **Capitalize the First Letter of Prepositions Over Three Letters Long, and Every Noun, Verb, Pronoun, Adjective, Adverb, and Subordinating Conjunction. (recommended)**
>
> **Capitalize the First Letter of Every Word Except Internal Articles and Prepositions.**
>
> **Capitalize only the first letter of the first word.**
>
> **Capitalize The First Letter Of Every Word.**
>
> **CAPITALIZE EVERY LETTER.**

Despite all the options, I learned the hard way that Grammar Girl readers have an overwhelming preference for the first option, which can also be stated as capitalize everything except *a, an, and, at, but, by, for, in, nor, of, on, or, so, the, to, up,* and *yet.* The original version of the Grammar Girl website used a different style, and boy, did I hear about it.

CAPITALIZATION, HYPHENS, AND TITLES

Hyphenated title words present you with a tricky choice. Do you capitalize the part after the hyphen or not? Again, it's a style issue. Some style guides say to capitalize the second part of a compound if it has the same weight or importance as the first part of the compound or if it is a noun, and other style guides say to make the second part lowercase if the word is always hyphenated.

The best thing to do is pick a style and stick with it. I capitalize the part after the hyphen if it would be capitalized without the hyphen.

Green-Bean Casserole Reported Missing

Worker Fired for Writing Run-on Sentence

AARDVARK, PRESIDENT OF SEATTLE: THE OTHER KIND OF TITLES

People usually obtain titles through hard work, birth, or imagination, but regardless of the method by which they gained the title, the titled class are often persnickety. So it's important to get the formatting right if you want to keep your head off the chopping block.

To make things harder for us lowly commoners, sometimes you capitalize titles and sometimes you don't.

In general, titles that come before names and are part of a title are capitalized, and titles that come after names are not capitalized. The key distinction you have to make is whether the word is part of an official title (in which case it is capitalized) or a descriptor (in which case it is lowercased). Common titles include *emperor, president, mayor, director,* and *chairperson.*

> **We invited *President Aardvark* to dinner.**
>
> ***Aardvark, president of Seattle,* came to dinner.**
>
> ***The president* came to dinner.**

Sometimes a title may come directly before the name but still be lowercased because it is a descriptor instead of part of the name:

> **Seattle president Aardvark Blueback came over for dinner.**

Sometimes writers ignore these rules; for example, writers may capitalize titles when they are creating a bulletin board or graduation program that includes many people with titles after their names.

Similarly, if you have the pleasure of addressing a knight, *sir* is capitalized. But if you are addressing someone who is not a knight, *sir* is lowercased.

> ***Sir Fragalot Franklin* has a problem making complete sentences.**
>
> ***Sir Fragalot,* please repeat the sentence.**
>
> **Please repeat the sentence, *sir.***

God Bless Grammar Girl: Religious Terms

The reason you aren't sure whether to capitalize *god* and *he* (when *he* refers to *god*) is that in some cases it's a style issue.

Of course, like any other proper noun, when *god* is the name of one specific god, it is capitalized, and when the word refers to multiple gods or is used as a descriptor it is lowercased:

Christians believe *God* is omniscient.

Stories about the *Greek gods* provide great inspiration for modern fiction.

***The god Apollo* is often shown playing the lyre.**

But less straightforward examples tend to vary with the religiosity of the publication. For example, newspapers tend to lowercase words that include *god,* such as *godsend* and *godlike,* whereas religious publications, tend to uppercase these words out of respect for God.

Similarly, most secular publications lowercase the pronoun *he* when it refers to God, but many religious publications uppercase the pronoun *he* out of respect.

In God we trust; *he* hasn't let us down yet. (secular)

In God we trust; *He* hasn't let us down yet. (religious)

There isn't a right answer; it simply depends on your audience.

WOOF AND MEOW: BREEDS

When in doubt about whether to capitalize a breed name, consult a dictionary. But in general, capitalize words derived from proper nouns and lowercase words derived from common nouns:

English mastiff

Yorkshire terrier

British shorthair

Havana brown

ragdoll

beagle

WANDERING THE FOUR CORNERS OF THE EARTH: DIRECTIONS

Direction names are lowercase when they describe a direction and uppercase when they describe a specific place (just like other proper nouns):

> **Go *southeast* until you reach the mall, then head west.**
>
> **He moved from *the South* to *the Midwest*.**
>
> **He's from *southern France*.**
>
> **He's from *South Korea*.**

TURN, TURN, TURN: DAYS, MONTHS, AND SEASONS

Days of the week and names of months are capitalized, but seasons are lowercased (unless they are part of a proper name).

> **Last *November* we had the *winter* dance on a *Friday*.**
>
> **The *2010 Winter Olympics* will be in Vancouver.**

FROM NOON TO MIDNIGHT

There are multiple acceptable ways to abbreviate *ante meridiem* and *post meridiem*.

American style is often to use small capital letters with periods after each letter and no space in between: A.M. and P.M. Using small capitals without periods is an acceptable alternative: AM and PM.

Because I can't figure out how to make small capitals in my e-mail program or on the website, I prefer the British method, which uses lowercase letters followed by periods: *a.m.* and *p.m.*

THE GRAMMAR GIRL ERA

Eras and time periods with specific names are capitalized:

Pliocene era

Romantic period

Middle Ages

Roaring Twenties

THE CAPITOL, THE CONGRESS, AND THE CONSTITUTION

In the United States, when the word *capitol* refers to the specific capitol building in Washington, D.C., it is capitalized: *Capitol, U.S. Capitol.* When it refers to the specific capitol building of a state or a complex of buildings, it is lowercased: *capitol.* (See page 20 for a discussion of *capitol* versus *capital.*) Similarly, *Congress* is capitalized when it refers to the U.S. Senate and House of Representatives or a specific session of the U.S. legislative body: *He spoke before the 22nd Congress. He's speaking before Congress today.* The adjective *congressional* is lowercased.

The word *Constitution* is capitalized when it is used to refer to the United States Constitution. However, the adjective *constitutional* is lowercased. The names of other historical documents, treaties, proclamations, bills, and acts are also capitalized: *Magna Carta, Treaty of Versailles, Declaration of Independence, First Amendment, Bill of Rights, Patriot Act,* and so on.

Chapter 6

PROZAC FOR PRONOUNS:
GETTING THE STUNTMEN OF LANGUAGE UNDER CONTROL

PRONOUNS ARE WORDS THAT STAND IN for nouns. They're pros, like stuntmen. When Aardvark, Squiggly, and Grammar Girl are feeling overworked, they call in a pronoun. Because pronouns don't get the same recognition as the big stars, they're a little temperamental. It's their way of getting even.

YOU AND I ARE GOING TO THE BEACH

Some pronouns will only work when they can be the subject, and other pronouns will only work when they can be the object. Remember, subjects are the ones taking action in a sentence and objects are the ones having action taken on them. For example, *I* is exclusively a subject pronoun, whereas *me* is exclusively an object pronoun.

I threw the beach ball.

(*I is the subject taking the action.*)

Squiggly threw me.

(*Me is the object getting thrown.*)

On the other hand, *you* is the low man on the totem pole. He has to stand in for everyone! *You* gets called to the set whether the script calls for a subject or an object.

You threw the beach ball.

(*You is the subject taking the action.*)

Squiggly threw you.

(*You is the object getting thrown.*)

You also fills in for one person or many people (i.e., it's a singular and a plural pronoun). If I say, "You should go to Disneyland," I could be talking to one person or a group of people. *You* could be standing in for Squiggly alone or Squiggly, Aardvark, and Sir Fragalot. It can be confusing, which is why people have created informal regional substitutes for the plural *you* such as *y'all, you guys,* and *youse.* Poor "you" needs to join a union!

THEY COME OVER FOR THE COMPANY, NOT THE FOOD

For some reason, people go all atwitter when company comes over. They clean things they haven't cleaned in months, buy expensive wine, and tend to cook enough food for an army. Similarly, many literate people who know how to behave when they are alone get flustered when other people show up in their sentences.

Is there really anyone reading this book who would say, "Me love Squiggly" instead of "I love Squiggly"? Yet throw in a third party and I

Pronoun Table

	Singular	Plural
Subject	You	You
	I	We
	He	They
	She	
	It	
	They*	
Object		
	You	You
	Me	Us
	Him	Them
	Her	
	It	
	Them*	

*Some grammarians, including me, allow people to use "they" and "them" as a singular pronoun when the sex of the subject is unknown.

bet some of you would say, "Your father and me love Squiggly." *Your father and me love Squiggly* is wrong for the same reasons that *Me love Squiggly* is wrong: you're putting an object pronoun (*me*) in the subject position. The correct sentence uses the subject pronoun in the subject position: *Your father and I love Squiggly*. So you can analyze subject and object if you want to, but the quick and dirty tip is to consider how you would write the sentence if you were in it alone.

People have the same problem when two or more people become the object in a sentence. Would any of you really say, "Father loves he"? I hope not! You'd correctly say, "Father loves him." But again, a younger sibling is born and suddenly everyone forgets how to construct a sentence. It's not *Father loves he and Squiggly*. Remember: object pronouns go in the object position. *Father loves him and Squiggly* is correct.

JUST BETWEEN YOU AND ME, YOU AND I KNOW HOW TO HAVE FUN

Sometimes even people who can deal with crowds in their sentences get confused when *you* shows up. (Hasn't he joined a union yet?)

The reason it gets a little tricky when you combine other pronouns with *you* is we have to remember that *you* is both a subject and an object pronoun. You love Squiggly, and Squiggly loves you. You and he should go scuba diving, and I went scuba diving with you and her. They are all correct.

So now that we've got our pronouns straight we can move on to *between you and I* and figure out why it's wrong. *Between* is a preposition, just as *at, above, over,* and *including* are prepositions. Because prepositions usually either describe a relationship or show possession, they don't act alone; they often answer questions like *Where?* and *When?* For example, if I said, "Keep that secret between you and me," *between* describes where the secret is to be kept. If I said, "I'll tell you the secret at Disneyworld," *at* describes where the secret will be revealed.

So, instead of acting alone, prepositions are part of prepositional phrases. In those example sentences, *between you and me* and *at Disneyworld* are prepositional·phrases. And it's just a rule that pronouns following prepositions in those phrases are always in the objective case. When you're using the objective case, the correct pronoun is *me,* so the correct prepositional phrase is *between you and me.*

Most grammarians are sympathetic to people who say "between you and I" because it's considered a hypercorrection.

(The theory is that people have been so traumatized by being corrected when they say things such as "Ashley and me went to the mall" instead of "Ashley and I went to the mall" that they incorrectly "correct" *between you and me* to *between you and I.*) If it helps, you can remember that Jessica Simpson's song "Between You and I" is wrong. I don't have anything against her. If remembering that her song is wrong helps you remember the rule, she's done a service to the world.

DANCING WITH *MYSELF*

Some people seem afraid to use the word *me*. Another hypercorrection that avoids *me* (like *between you and I*) is throwing *myself* into a sentence when you are unsure or want to sound refined.

Let's dissect what's wrong with this sentence: *Please contact Aardvark or myself with questions.* Once more you've run into the problem of having multiple people in the sentence. Step back and consider how you would say the sentence without Aardvark. Then it usually becomes obvious—you would say, "Please contact me with questions," not, "Please contact myself with questions." So when you add in Aardvark it doesn't change anything. It's still correct to say, "Please contact Aardvark or me with questions."

Myself is what's called a reflexive pronoun. Just think about looking into a mirror and seeing your reflection. You'd say, "I see myself in the mirror." You see your reflection, and *myself* is called a reflexive pronoun.

Other reflexive pronouns include *himself, herself, yourself, itself, ourselves,* and *themselves.* A reflexive pronoun can only be the object of a sentence; it can never be the subject. You would never say, "Myself stepped on Squiggly" (because *myself* is incorrectly used as the subject), so you would also never say, "Aardvark and myself stepped on Squiggly."

The reflexive pronoun is the right choice when the subject is mentioned again in the sentence. For example, you can use *myself* when you are both the subject and the object of a sentence: "I see myself playing maracas" or "I'm going to treat myself to a mud bath." In both of these cases you are the object of your own action, so *myself* is the right word to use.

Reflexive pronouns can also be used to add emphasis to a sentence. (In case you care, they are then called intensive pronouns.) For example, if you saw a stuntman crash on the set, you could say, "I myself saw the horrible crash." Sure, it's a tad dramatic, but it's grammatically correct. If you want to emphasize how proud you are of the twelve-course meal you cooked for your dinner guests, you could say, "I prepared the dinner myself." Again, *myself* just adds emphasis. The meaning of the sentence doesn't change if you take out the word *myself*; it just has a different feeling because now it lacks the added emphasis.

It Is I, Grammar Girl

It is I. (proper)

It is me. (acceptable)

Once you get past the age where the only people who call you are your friends, you've probably wondered (at least in passing) whether you should respond, "That is me" or "That is I" when someone calls and asks, "Is_____home?"

The short answer is that it's proper to respond, "That is I."

The traditional grammar rule states that when a pronoun follows a linking verb, such as *is*, it should be in the subject case. That means it is correct to say, "It is I" and "It was he who dropped the phone in shock when I answered, 'This is she.'"

Linking verbs are words such as *is, was, were, appear,* and *seem,* which don't describe an action so much as describe a state of being. (See pages 15 and 31 for further discussions of linking verbs and page 198 for a list of common linking verbs.) When pronouns follow these non–action verbs, you use the subject pronouns such as *I, she, he, they,* and *we.*

Here are some additional correct examples:

Who called Squiggly? It was he.

Who told you about it? It was I.

Who had the phone conversation? It must have been they.

Who cares? It is we.

Now the problem is that 90 percent of you are almost certainly thinking, "That all sounds really weird. Is she serious?" Well, yes, I'm serious, and that is the traditional rule, but fortunately most grammarians forgive you for not following the rule because it sounds stilted and fussy, even to us.

So if you're the kind of person who prefers to be proper, it's fine to say, "That is I," and if you prefer to be more casual, it's fine to say, "That is me."

On a related note, people often wonder which pronoun to use after words such as *than* and *as.* For example, is it *Squiggly wants to go to Disneyworld more than I/me* and *Squiggly isn't as tall as I/me*?

The answer is similar to the answer in the case of *it is I.*

Traditional grammar rules state that you use the subject pronoun (in this case, *I*) after words such as *than* and *as.* The sentence is considered to be short for *Squiggly wants to go to Disneyworld more than I (want to go),* and *Squiggly isn't as tall as I (am).* But again, using the object pronoun, *me,* is so common that most grammarians also accept it in these situations. Some people even argue that *than* and *as* are being used as prepositions instead of conjunctions in these kinds of sentences, which would make *me* acceptable. Since there are reasonable arguments on both sides, which pronoun you choose (*I* or *me*) says more about your personality than anything else (formal or informal).

I hate it when language is in flux like this because it's easy to get confused. But a lot of people have asked me these questions, and in the end, I believe it's best to know the traditional rules. If you decide to break them, you can do so knowingly and with conviction.

ORDERING NOUNS AND PRONOUNS IN A SENTENCE

It's a matter of politeness, not grammar, that leads people to put themselves last in a list. In the same way that you hold a door open to let others walk through first, you should let everyone else go first in your sentences.

So the song titles "Me and Julio Down by the Schoolyard," and "Me and Bobby McGee" would be considered impolite (and they're sentence fragments).

Even when you're using the possessive pronoun *my,* you put yourself last in the list: *Aardvark's and my car is in the shop.*

Speaking of Politeness: Malapropisms

"He's the very pineapple of politeness," is a line from the Richard Sheridan play *The Rivals* in which Mrs. Malaprop habitually mixes up words to make malapropisms. What she meant to say is, "He's the very pinnacle of politeness."

Malapropism is derived from a French phrase meaning "badly for the purpose." Malapropisms occur when someone substitutes a similar-sounding word for another word. In another example of a malapropism, U.S. president George W. Bush, who is known for his misspeaks, in 2003 was reported to say, "nucular power pants" instead of "nuclear power plants."

While we're on the subject of sentence fragments, people often wonder how they should write photo captions. Should it be *Bobby McGee and Me* or *Bobby McGee and I?*

Captions are just another name for nothin' left to lose. No. Wait. What I meant to say is that captions with just names aren't sentences, they're sentence fragments, so it's awkward to try to apply grammar rules to them in the first place. You have to imagine what they would mean if they were in a sentence. Are you implying *It was good enough for Bobby McGee and me* or *This is Bobby McGee and I in Baton Rouge*?

You learned in the "It is I" section that even though I wrote that second sentence the proper way (*Bobby McGee and I*), it would also be acceptable in most cases to write "This is Bobby McGee and *me* in Baton Rouge." So when forced to choose, I believe it is better to caption your photos *Bobby McGee and me* instead of *Bobby McGee and I*. Whew! That was a lot of explaining to end up saying the lyrics are on the right track.

Chapter 7
INTERNET INTERVENTION

THE GENERAL PUBLIC DIDN'T START using the Internet until the National Center for Supercomputing Applications released the Mosaic Web browser in 1993, and even then you could hardly call users the general public—students and serious tech geeks would be more accurate. (I was both, thank you!) Even though I lived before the Internet, I can't imagine life without it anymore. Nevertheless, along with all the power and wonder came a great gnashing of teeth as writers (and programmers) tried to wrangle this new stuff onto a page. Building new conventions takes time, and even though we've now had about fifteen years to sort it out, much of what I can offer you are still just recommendations—style—rather than hard-and-fast rules.

BRAVE NEW WORDS

With so many new things to talk about, it's no surprise that a lot of new words emerged to talk about them. Some words are completely new (*Internet*), some are old words that take on a new meaning (*zombie*, a computer that is taken over by hackers), and some activities are referred to with competing words or phrases (*log in, log on*). Here are a few of the words I am asked about most frequently.

LOG ME IN, COACH; I'M READY TO PLAY: *LOG IN* VERSUS *LOG ON*

Log in, log on, log out, and *log off* are all considered phrasal verbs. In other words, they are two-word verbs. *Log in* and *log on* are interchangeable, as are *log out* and *log off*. In certain cases, the two parts of the word can be split: *She logged Grammar Girl off the system.*

If you use these words as adjectives (for example before a noun), use a hyphen: *I hate the flashing graphics on the log-in page.*

ON LINE VERSUS *ONLINE*

Online is all one word. When you're on the Internet, you're online; and when you're buying stuff on eBay, you're conducting an online transaction. (There's a separate discussion about people saying they are standing on line instead of in line in chapter 1, "Dirty Words.")

NO MATTER WHAT BUSH SAYS, IT'S NOT CALLED THE INTERNETS

Remember from the capitalization chapter (chapter 5) that words are capitalized because they are proper nouns, not because they are important or new.

So to understand why we capitalize *Internet* (or not), we have to decide whether the Internet is one specific thing or not. Most language experts believe the Internet is one big but specific thing—when you talk about the Internet, there is only one thing you could be referring to—so *Internet* is a proper noun and gets capitalized.

Web, which is short for "World Wide Web," is also generally considered to be one specific thing, so it also gets capitalized. I've heard the arguments that it looks antiquated to capitalize *Internet* or that the Internet isn't special anymore so it shouldn't be capitalized, but those arguments miss the underlying grammatical rationale for why we capitalize words in English.

On the other hand, *Web site* or *website* is trickier. There are hundreds of millions of websites on the Web. If you use the open compound (*Web site*), the Web part gets capitalized, because *Web* is still a proper noun, but *site* is not. If you close the compound (*website*), the entire word is a common noun because it is not a name for one specific thing, so it is lowercased.

Whether you use the open or closed compound comes down to a matter of style; *Web site* is nearly twice as common on the Internet as *website*. (A Google search for "Web site" yielded approximately 1.6 billion hits, whereas a search for "website" yielded approximately 0.9 billion hits.)

Bear in mind that many people use *Internet* and *Web* interchangeably, but they are two separate things. (I made this error myself once in a Grammar Girl podcast and boy, did I hear about it!)

The Internet is an international network of computers that use the IP and TCP protocols to find each other and exchange information. Protocols such as HTTP and FTP run on the Internet.

The World Wide Web (Web) is made up of all the files that are accessible on the Internet by using the HTTP protocol.

MAY I HAVE YOUR ADDRESS?: UNIVERSAL RESOURCE LOCATORS (URLs)

Web addresses are strange beasts; they seem more like equations or long numbers than words. All the rules for how to handle uniform resource locators (URLs) in documents are matters of style, but some styles make more sense than others.

The Information Superhighway

An argument for not capitalizing *Internet* is to use the National Highway System as an analogy for the Internet. Much like the Internet, the National Highway System is a network of interconnected lines—traffic lines instead of data lines. *National Highway System* is capitalized because it is a proper noun that refers to one big network, yet when I write "Let's take the highway," *highway* isn't capitalized because I'm using the word *highway* as a common noun to refer to a small part of the National Highway System. I'm thinking about hopping onto I-80, whereas someone in Seattle could use *highway* to refer to I-5, and someone in New York could use *highway* to refer to I-84. The reason the National Highway System is not a perfect analogy for the Internet is that different lines of the Internet aren't named and in the public consciousness in the same way as individual sections of the National Highway System. When someone in New York and someone in California talk about "getting on the Internet," they are both thinking of the same entity.

URLs and Terminal Punctuation

URLs always have internal periods and often are scattered with other punctuation marks too, so what do you do when one shows up at the end of a sentence? Should you include the period or other terminal punctuation mark at the end of the sentence as you normally would, leave off the period so the reader doesn't mistakenly include it in the address, or do something funky such as put quotes around the Web address? As you're weighing your options, first consider whether you are writing online or in print.

Print

If you're writing for print, Web addresses don't need special treatment. Put the period, question mark, etc., at the end of the sentence just as you would if the sentence ended with a word or a number. You may choose to highlight the URL in some way, such as making it bold or blue, but it isn't necessary.

Online

When you're writing a URL in a blog, e-mail program, or other on-line environment and the link will be active, you have to be sure the terminal punctuation won't be included in the address when someone clicks on it or quickly copies it and pastes it into their browser. Many e-mail and instant messaging programs, for example, automatically make everything following *http://* active until a space is reached—meaning the terminal punctuation will be included in the address, resulting in a broken link. Thus, unless you can control exactly how the address will be rendered, it's best to leave off the terminal punctuation. (I know! It makes me crazy to leave off the punctuation too, but I've had enough people complain that a link I posted or sent them didn't work that I've changed my mind and decided that functionality beats traditional sentence structure.)

The Full Monte: Full URLs Versus Abbreviated URLs

Some people prefer to write out the entire address including the *http://* and *www* parts, whereas other people prefer to write the shortest address that will still work when you type it into a Web browser. Whether you should write out the full URL is also a matter of style, but for the reasons that follow, I recommend writing out the complete address every time.

- Most—but importantly, not all—websites will come up in a browser if you leave off the *http://www*. If you opt to use an abbreviated address, always test it in a browser first; don't assume it will work.

- Not every address uses *www*. For example, the direct Grammar Girl Web address is http://grammar.quickanddirtytips.com. It's best to include the *http://* in these kinds of addresses because people may be confused if you just write *grammar.quickanddirtytips.com* and try to insert a *www.* in front of it.

The bottom line is that although an abbreviated address may look smoother and more tech savvy, it's not going to work every time, so you're going to end up writing the *http://* sometimes. Since you have to write it sometimes, it makes your style more consistent to use it all the time.

Long URLs

The next problem you are likely to encounter is what to do with a long URL. You know what I mean: one of those dynamically generated URLs that seem to go on forever with equal signs and question marks and lots of numbers.

The most important thing is that if you have to break a URL across two lines, don't insert an extra hyphen at the line break. That will definitely confuse people because it's common for URLs to have internal hyphens. And if there is a hyphen in the address, don't make the line break right after it; that will confuse people because they won't know whether you are improperly inserting a hyphen to mark the break or the hyphen is part of the address.

Instead, if you have to wrap the URL to a new line, find a natural break like a slash, a number sign, or other symbol. Again, use common sense: don't break a URL right after a period or readers may think the period marks the end of the sentence. If you must break at a period, make the break before the period so it starts the new line.

http://www.stumbleupon.com/submit?url=
http://grammar.quickanddirtytips.com/af
fect-versus-effect.aspx&title = Effect + Versus + Affect
(right because it breaks between letters)

**http://www.stumbleupon.com/submit?url = http://
grammar.quickanddirtytips.
com/affect-versus-effect.aspx&title = Effect + Versus + Affect**

(wrong because it breaks at a terminal punctuation mark)

**http://www.stumbleupon.com/submit?url = http://
grammar.quickanddirtytips.com/affect-
versus-effect.aspx&title = Effect + Versus + Affect**

(wrong because it breaks at a hyphen)

Active Links

Some word processing programs annoyingly make a link active when you type the full address. I find that almost as annoying as Clippy, the old Microsoft pop-up helper. If your document will only be read in print, there's no reason to make the link active; it will just show up underlined in the printout, which is unnecessary. You can remove the link by following the instructions in the sidebar.

On the other hand, if your document will be on the Web or in an e-mail message, do make the link clickable so it's easier for your readers to visit the page.

Removing Active Hyperlinks

How to remove the active hyperlink in an Open Office document on a PC or a Mac:

1. **Highlight the text.**
2. **In the Format menu, choose Character (or hit the key sequence Alt-O-H on a PC).**

> **3. In the Hyperlink tab, delete any text in the URL box.**
> **4. Hit OK.**
>
> How to remove the active hyperlink in an MS Word document on a PC or a Mac:
>
> **1. Put your cursor anywhere on the link.**
> **2. Press Control-K (Command-K for a Mac) to bring up the Edit Hyperlink menu.**
> **3. Click Remove Link in the bottom left corner of the menu.**

Click Here and Underlining

When you're turning words into links on a Web page, apply the link to the words that best describe the destination page. For example, link the words *Grammar Girl Homepage* instead of linking generic words such as *click here*. Using meaningful link text also helps your site rank well in search engines and makes it easier for people with visual impairments to navigate your site. (They may be using software that reads only the link text to them.)

Also, it's best to avoid underlining things for emphasis on websites because underlining is the style for hyperlinks on the Web. I know it's possible to make links any style you want if you fiddle with the code, but underlining is the default style, so if you underline text, some people will think it's an active link.

CAMELCASE

CamelCase (also known as medial capitals, intercaps, humpbacking, CapWords, and BiCapitals, among other names) is the practice, that has now become trendy, of promoting a letter in the middle of a word to uppercase. Most often the medial capital letter seems to result from squishing two words together that would normally be separated by a space (e.g., PageMaker), but occasionally the capital just seems to pop up at a convenient syllable (e.g., OutKast).

Leave the camel at the zoo.

Although the phenomenon can be traced back to at least the '50s, it gained steam among computer programmers (probably because spaces are often discouraged or disallowed in programming) and then caught on with marketers as a trendy way to make a company name stand out.

If a formal company name uses CamelCase (e.g., MySpace, YouTube, PayPal, TiVo), use that form in your writing. But other than honoring official names, leave the camel at the zoo—don't go around calling a plain old help desk a HelpDesk. It's just so unnecessary!

E-MAIL DOES NOT STAND FOR EVIL-MAIL: SOME SIMPLE SUGGESTIONS FOR IMPROVING YOUR E-MAIL MESSAGES

Today, everyone is a writer. In the past people picked up the phone and called each other, but now we are more likely to write an e-mail or text message. It's not uncommon to spend hours (and thousands of written words) swapping messages with colleagues or customers you hardly ever talk to and may never meet. Your e-mail messages are often the primary means people use to form their opinions about you. Are you stuffy? smart? fun? considerate? professional? Your e-mail messages need to have a metaphorical firm handshake and be dressed for success if you want to get ahead in today's world.

Formal or Informal

Questions about e-mail often get me thinking about overarching language rules and how they depend on whether a specific situation is formal or informal. For example, people have asked me if it's OK to start a sentence with a conjunction such as *and* or *but,* and my answer is that it's OK in informal settings but should be avoided in formal settings. Similarly, when you're writing an e-mail message, take a second to think about the purpose of your writing. Is it formal or informal?

- **A formal setting** is something such as a cover letter for a job application, a letter to a client, a book report for school, or an e-mail message to a new client or your boss' boss' boss.

- **An informal setting** is something such as an e-mail message to a friend, something you would say in casual conversation, or a text message.

- **Some things fall in the middle;** you have to just use your own judgment. Is a text message to your boss a formal or informal communication? Only you can decide. It depends on your corporate culture and relationship with your boss, but if there is any doubt, it's better to assume it's formal.

You wouldn't begin an e-mail message to a professor with "Hey, Dude"—please, tell me you wouldn't!—so it's not too hard to figure out that you probably shouldn't write to your boss that you're sorry you're L8 to the mtg & will brb. (For the uninitiated, you're sorry you're late to the meeting and will be right back.)

The Subject Line

I have received countless e-mail messages that bear no relation to the subject line or that refer to some vague meeting or decision I can't decipher. It makes me wonder: does the author only attend one meeting each week, make one decision per month, or never have to go back and find a message later? I call this a context problem.

It's often easier (and more appropriate) to reply to a message than to compose a message from scratch without including the old messages that came before your response, but when you reply, e-mail programs automatically insert the same subject line text with an *RE:* in front of it. If your topic drifts over time, you can end up sending a message that is completely unrelated to the subject line. Although you are writing about meeting for dinner after the conference, the subject line may read "Revisions to the revenue slide."

The first problem with the mismatch is that your readers are expecting something other than what they get when they open the message, and the second problem is that if you have to go back later and look for messages you sent about the revenue slide, you'll have to look through a bunch of garbage about the dinner.

The quick and dirty tip is to make sure your subject line matches the message content.

WHEN A "DEAR JOHN" LETTER BECOMES A "HI, JOHN" LETTER

Now that you've written a meaningful subject line, it's time to write the salutation. You've probably never even thought about this, but technically those messages you're writing should begin *Hi, John*—with a comma after *Hi.* You see, *Hi, John* is actually different from *Dear John* because *hi* and *dear* are not the same kinds of words. *Hi* is an imperative, and *dear* is an adjective that modifies *John.* In *Hi, John* you are directly addressing John, which means the punctuation rules of direct address apply. From a comma-rules standpoint, *Hi, John* is no different from *Thank you for the flowers, John.*

This is a tough one though. The rules are clear, but in the real world almost nobody follows them. I estimate that less than 1 in 10,000 e-mail messages I receive use the comma correctly. People seem to think *dear* sounds too formal and they can swap in *hi* to be more friendly, so I end up feeling pedantic and stuffy when I do it right, especially when I am responding to someone who has already left out the comma. On the other hand, I also feel a moral obligation to set a good example.

You have to use your own judgment on this one and decide whether you want to be technically correct or go with common usage.

Dear John, (correct)

Hi, John. (correct)

Hi John, (common usage, but not technically correct)

Other Salutation Questions

The plural of *Mister* (*Mr.*) is *Messieurs* (*Messrs.*). It is common to use abbreviations when writing a letter, so if you were writing to multiple men, this is the correct way to format your salutation: *Dear Messrs. Affleck and Pitt.*

The plural of *Mrs.* is *Mmes.* (short for *Mesdames*), and the plural of *Miss* is *Misses*. The plural of *Ms.*, which originated in the 1950s, is less clear. Various sources report that the plural of *Ms.* can be *Mses.*, *Mss.*, or *Mmes.*

In American English, a period is required after the abbreviations; in British English, no punctuation is required after the abbreviations.

Context

Like writing a meaningful subject line, it is a good idea to give your reader context in the actual e-mail message. Even if you include the text of every previous message that led to your message, don't force your reader to sift through it all to figure out what you mean. Spell it out for them. It doesn't take much extra time to write, "Here is the revenue slide with the new chart you requested," instead of "Here it is."

Formatting

Have you ever noticed how much harder it is to read a thousand-word message with long paragraphs than a twenty-word message or a long message that is broken up into short paragraphs? Give some thought to how you format your message. Reading on a computer screen is different from reading on paper, and a long, text-dense e-mail message is just as hard to read as a long, text-dense Web page. If you can't distill your message down to one or two short paragraphs, consider using the same formatting tricks that make websites easier to read:

- **Use bulleted lists when possible.**

- **Use subheadings to separate different sections of your message.**

- **Use bold formatting to highlight the most important points in your message** such as the first sentence of each paragraph or first point in your bulleted list, as I've done here.

- **Use regular capitalization and punctuation.** Writing with all capital letters is the equivalent of shouting, and not capitalizing the first word of a sentence is lazy and makes it look as if you don't care about your reader or your message. Also, don't overdo ellipses. (See pages 109–111 for further discussion of ellipses in e-mail messages.)

Sign-offs and Signatures

Sincerely or *Regards* are good formal sign offs for business letters to people you don't know well or don't correspond with often, but *Sincerely* can sound too formal for someone you write to regularly. On the other hand, *Cheers* and *Later* are quite informal and should be reserved for people you feel very comfortable with, and *Namaste, Love, Hugs,* and *Yours Truly* are quite intimate and should be reserved for close friends or family. If you are in extreme doubt about which closing to use, it is acceptable to leave out the closing in e-mail and simply sign with your name or e-mail signature. Also, it is customary to leave off the closing in messages to people you correspond with frequently.

An e-mail signature should consist minimally of your full name and a way to contact you—ideally a phone number and an e-mail address. Even if you write to people regularly and you think they have your contact information, it is polite to include it so they don't have to look it up if they want to contact you while they are reading your message. It's also fine to include a physical address or Web address in your signature, but don't make your signature an overwhelming marketing message that contains everything from your work projects to personal blogs and social networking links. (It may be necessary to have different signatures for different parts of your life; for example, you may need a work signature, a family signature, and a personal projects signature if you want different people to contact you in different ways or you want to highlight different projects.)

P.S. I Love You

P.S. is an abbreviation for the Latin words *post scriptum,* which mean "after writing." A P.S. has traditionally been used to add a thought after the writer has finished writing the main body of a letter. Because it is so easy to go back and edit an e-mail, some people object to using the P.S. format in e-mail. Despite these objections, a P.S. can serve a legitimate purpose in an e-mail message, particularly in denoting that the statement is an afterthought and perhaps unrelated to the main point of the e-mail message. On the other hand, it is conceivable that occasionally readers will miss reading the P.S. because they will fail to scroll down beyond the final signature.

Although it is common to see additional levels of *P.S.*'s written as *P.S.S.* and *P.S.S.S.,* they would be more correctly written as *P.P.S.* (*post post scriptum*) and *P.P.P.S.* (*post post post scriptum*). But the need for multiple layers of post scripting is a sure sign that your original message is not well conceived, and multiple post scripts should be avoided in all but the most informal writing. In short, more than one *P.S.* makes you look scatterbrained.

Unsend

There is no "unsend" button for e-mail. It's tempting to think that the message you are sending will only be seen by the person you are writing to; tempting, but not realistic. E-mail messages get forwarded, people accidentally hit the "reply to all" button instead of "reply," and people snoop on other people's computers. Before you hit Send, imagine how you would feel if your message were posted on the office refrigerator or shown to your mom. Make edits as necessary.

TEXT MESSAGING IS NOT BOOK WRITING

Formal or Informal

You don't need to completely abandon abbreviations such as *brb* (be right back) and *lol* (laughing out loud) for text messaging, but as with e-mail, you do need to be aware of the purpose of your writing. Is it formal or informal? What are the expectations of your recipient?

I checked with the Quick and Dirty Tips etiquette expert, the Modern Manners Guy, and he said it's rude to use text messaging abbreviations when the person on the receiving end won't understand them, but he said that it may also be rude *not* to use them when you are sending a message to someone who you know will understand the abbreviations and is reading your message on a tiny cell phone screen. If you write everything out, the recipient will have to do a lot more scrolling to read your message. Again, the underlying theme is to consider the specific situation.

Twitter

I'm not a big text messager (probably because I have a lame cell phone), but I do use Twitter, a Web social networking tool that lets me write posts about what I'm doing at any given time. I love how it helps me keep in touch with lots of people throughout the day while I'm working at my computer. If you use Twitter too, you can follow me directly. My username is GrammarGirl.

Twittering is a lot like text messaging because your entries are limited to 140 characters. (Similarly, the Facebook status message is limited to 161 characters and has the further restriction that it automatically begins with your name.) Sometimes I find it challenging to get my point across and still use proper grammar, spelling, and punctuation. But I'm Grammar Girl, so I have to! I was spending a lot of time trying to decide what was acceptable and what wasn't, and then I realized I needed a Twitter style guide. Fellow Twitterer Cathleen Ritteriser came up with the name: *Strunk & Twite*. The complete *Strunk & Twite* guide is in the appendix; I hope you'll read the guide and join me on Twitter!

ePain in the A**

God bless eBay—it's one of the few real success stories from the dot-com days, and who doesn't love to score a collectible Pez dispenser—but there's nothing I hate more than facing a sentence that starts with an eSomething (or an iSomething, for that matter. Hi, Steve Jobs!). What do you do when a company insists that their name starts with a lowercase letter? This is a style issue, and a contentious one at that. Many editors hold firm that the first letter of a sentence should be capitalized regardless of what companies prefer. Alternatively, companies themselves start sentences with the lowercase letter to support their trademark and branding (eBay reported record earnings . . .), and many readers (including me) find it jarring to see a name like *iPod* rendered *Ipod*. It just looks wrong!

Although I've heard editors complain about arrogant companies and their %(#@*$ lowercase names, the problem isn't limited to brand names. You can also run across the problem in other areas such as chemistry (e.g., *pH*), surnames (e.g., *de Heer, van Bern*), and computing (where variable names may be case sensitive).

The best solution is always to rewrite the sentence so the offending word isn't at the beginning. As a backup, you should select a house style for instances where a rewrite isn't possible. It's like choosing a selling price for a stock in advance—make the decision about how you will handle the situation with a cool head instead of in the heat of the moment.

ARE YOU GOING TO CITE ME FOR THAT?: CITING A WEBSITE

Risks

Citing a website can be dangerous. First, you have to determine whether it's a credible source, and second, you have to worry about whether it will still exist tomorrow.

Determining whether a source is credible can be subjective, but here are a few things to look for and consider:

- **Can you tell who wrote the site?** And if so, do they seem to have any expertise in the area you are researching. The Stanford Cancer Center is a more credible source than Aunt Mary's Kancer Page.

- **Has the website been reviewed by experts; does it bear a seal of approval or adhere to content standards?** For example, health sites wanting to boost their credibility adhere to standards set by the Health on the Net Foundation.

- **Can you tell when the page you are looking at was written?** Something written recently is generally more credible than something that hasn't been updated in years.

- **Does the page cite other credible sources you can check?**

- **Does it sound too good to be true?** If it does, it probably is.

- **Are they selling something based on the information the site is providing?** If so, be wary.

- **Do other credible sites link to the site?** You can find out who links to a site by doing a specialized search on Google. Enter *link: URL* into the search box. For example, you could enter *link:* http://www .genetichealth.com (a website I helped launch) and find out that sites that link to it include a Japanese genome center, the Lance Armstrong Foundation, and a variety of hospitals.

- **Are there a lot of typos?** If there are a lot of language mistakes, it can mean that there are a lot of factual mistakes too.

Finally, use common sense and evaluate the arguments yourself. It's up to you to determine whether a site's conclusions are actually supported by its statements.

Pages disappearing or changing their Web address are problems that are out of your control. If it is an important source, you should consider printing out the page or saving it on your own computer. If you find that a page is gone and you haven't had a chance to save it yourself, you can sometimes find it at the Internet Archive (also known as the Wayback Machine) at http://web.archive.org.

Despite the risks, an abundance of credible information resides on the Web and you shouldn't dismiss a source simply because it is in a convenient electronic format.

Formatting

If you're including a Web address in a list of references and you're using a specific referencing style like that of the Modern Language Association, American Psychological Association, or *The Chicago Manual of Style,* then follow their specific recommendations; but if you're writing an essay or e-mail message, the style is up to you (or your boss or teacher). Just be consistent.

Modern Language Association

Fogarty, Mignon. "Affect Versus Effect." <u>Quick and Dirty Tips Website</u>. 14 Oct. 2006. <http://grammar.quickanddirtytips.com/affect-versus-effect.aspx>.

American Psychological Association

Fogarty, M. (2006, October 14). Affect Versus Effect. *Quick and Dirty Tips Website*. Retrieved November 15, 2007, from http://grammar.quickanddirtytips.com/affect-versus-effect.aspx

The Chicago Manual of Style

Fogarty, Mignon. "Affect Versus Effect," Quick and Dirty Tips Website, October 14, 2006, http://grammar.quickanddirtytips.com/affect-versus-effect.aspx (accessed November 15, 2007).

Chapter 8

I'M SO STYLISH:
STYLE AND WRITING

ALL WRITERS HAVE THEIR OWN style, and I don't believe style is something you can teach. Everyone's writing voice is as different as their speaking voice. (Yes, *everyone* is a singular noun, and I am still insisting on using *their* as a gender-neutral singular pronoun. Aren't you used to it by now?) I may be able to impersonate Steve Martin or Toni Morrison, but it would take hard work and concentration, whereas speaking or writing in my own voice comes naturally. It still requires hard work—some days writing is downright painful—but it does come naturally once it starts flowing.

So why did I even include a chapter on style if I don't think it can be taught? Well, the last seven chapters were about avoiding big mistakes. This chapter is about avoiding big annoyances. It's a step on the way to style, which in the end, you must find for yourself, grasshopper.

WORDINESS

Wordiness bugs people. If you don't believe me, I can show you the e-mail messages I get from listeners. The complaints I get about wordiness are often laced with serious venom. It's as if the complainer has been locked in a box and forced to listen to the same wordy phrase over and over again. Oh wait, isn't that the definition of office life?

For example, I found myself wondering if a listener named Tod, who complained about the wordy phrase *go ahead and,* works with someone like the annoying manager Bill Lumbergh in the movie *Office Space* who says things such as

> **If you want to, *go ahead and* wear a Hawaiian shirt and jeans.**
>
> **Are you going to *go ahead and* have those TPS reports for us this afternoon?**

Tod is right—Lumberghian phrases such as *go ahead and* are wordy and unnecessary. Many wordiness slips are easy to make in writing because we use them in speech to soften bad news or get people's attention. Here's one I'm guilty of: I'm always tempted to start e-mails with the phrase *I just want to let you know,* and then I get to my point. I always have to go back and rewrite my messages so I don't belittle my own sentiment and waste the reader's time. For example, I'll write, "I just wanted to let you know that I love your podcast." Ugh! Just say it: *Dear Money Girl, I love your podcast.* There's no need to sneak up on the sentence as if you're trying to lasso a wild horse!

On the other hand, sometimes wordiness can make bad news seem less harsh. *I thought you should know that Tom died last night* sounds less cold than *Tom died last night.*

Repetitive Redundancy

Redundancy is another common pet peeve, a subspecies of wordiness. If you don't think redundancy annoys people, consider my listener who angrily focused on the redundancy of this sign rather than the message: *Season's Greetings and Happy Holidays.* Don't tell him you love *and* adore him if you know what's good for you!

The reason . . . is because is another redundant phrase that sends people off the deep end because to say "the reason" implies "because." I know; I said it in my show once! Consider this sentence, and the two simplified versions that follow:

> **The reason you love grammar *is because* you love rules. (redundant)**
>
> **The reason you love grammar *is that* you love rules. (acceptable)**
>
> **You love grammar *because* you love rules. (better)**

You can be particularly tempted to write redundant acronyms and initialisms because you forget what the letters represent. For example, I was writing about a science experiment, and I found myself writing the phrase *PCR reaction;* and then I remembered that *PCR* stands for *polymerase chain reaction,* so I had just written *polymerase chain reaction reaction,* which is obviously redundant. Yet, I often hear people speak redundantly; they say such things as "I ran a PCR reaction." There's something about ending a sentence with an acronym that often sounds wrong, but adding redundant words doesn't make it any better.

Other examples of abbreviations that lure people into redundancy are *PIN* (*PIN number* is redundant because the *n* in *PIN* stands for *number,* so people are saying *personal identification number number*) and *HIV* (*HIV virus* is redundant because *v* stands for *virus*).

The important thing to remember is when you are using an acronym, take a second to think about the words it stands for so you don't add a redundant word at the end. If you are afraid people won't know what you mean if you use the acronym without the redundant word, then don't use the acronym—write out the whole thing.

Avoid Clichés Like the Plague

Phrases are like furniture. For a short time they are comfortable or even brilliant, but it doesn't take long for them to become shabby. Clichés are OK once in a blue moon, but the very definition of *cliché* argues against their use: "a trite, overused expression."

Overreliance on clichés can be a sign of weak writing because it usually means you couldn't think of a creative way to get your point across and instead you lazily borrowed a phrase someone else created years ago. Is avoiding someone like the plague really relevant today, or would it touch your readers' lives more if you said, "He's as welcome as a Nigerian spammer"? The next time you are tempted to write a cliché, think about how much you believe the checker at the grocery store wants you to "Have a nice day," and try again.

That Problem

People also get all riled up about the word *that*. It's redundant! Unnecessary! "Strike it wherever you can!" shout many editors. They've been driven to this madness by writers who use *that* with wild abandon.

Aardvark told her *that* she was the one *that* he wanted to go with.

(two unnecessary thats)

Aardvark told her she was the one he wanted to go with.

(better without the thats)

Unfortunately, many editors take their *that* phobia to extremes and delete *that*s even when the word is needed for clarity, as in the following example:

Aardvark maintains her yard is too large.

(almost certain to miscue the reader into initially thinking Aardvark mows her lawn)

Aardvark maintains *that* her yard is too large.

(clearer with the that *included)*

ACTIVE VOICE VERSUS PASSIVE VOICE

Passive voice is one of those things many people believe they should avoid, but fewer people can define.

I'll start with active voice because it's simpler. In an active sentence, the subject is doing the action. A straightforward example is the following sentence:

Squiggly loves Aardvark.

Squiggly is the subject, and he is doing the action: he loves Aardvark, the object. (See page 46 in chapter 1, "Dirty Words," for an overview of subject versus object.)

In passive voice, the target of the action gets promoted to the subject position. Instead of saying, "Squiggly loves Aardvark," I would say,

Aardvark is loved by Squiggly.

The subject of the sentence becomes Aardvark, but he isn't doing anything. Rather, he is just the recipient of Squiggly's love. The focus of the sentence has changed from Squiggly to Aardvark.

A lot of people think all sentences that contain a form of the verb *to be* are in passive voice, but that isn't true. For example, the sentence "I am holding a pen" is in active voice, but it uses the verb *am,* which is a form of *to be.* The passive form of that sentence is *The pen is being held by me.*

Another important point is that passive sentences aren't incorrect; often they just aren't the best way to phrase your thoughts. Sometimes passive voice is awkward and other times it's vague.

When you put sentences in passive voice, it's easy to leave out the person who is responsible for the action. For example, *Aardvark is loved* is passive. The problem with that sentence is you don't know who loves Aardvark. In fact, politicians often use passive voice to intentionally obscure the idea of who is taking the action. Ronald Reagan famously said, "Mistakes were made," when referring to the Iran-Contra scandal. Other examples of passive voice for political reasons could include *Bombs were dropped* and *Shots were fired*. Watch the news. Now that you're aware of the difference between active and passive voice, you'll hear politicians use passive voice almost every day.

So, the reasons to avoid passive voice are that the form can lead to awkward sentences and obscured meaning. Also, passive voice is wordy. You can tighten up your writing if you use active voice more often than passive voice.

On the other hand, there are instances where passive voice is the best choice. If you don't know who is taking the action, then you can't name that person. Depending on the context, it may make more sense to write "*The cookies* were stolen" instead of "*Somebody* stole the cookies." It's a subtle difference. If you want to put the focus on the cookies—for example, if you are writing a mystery novel and you want to highlight the cookies because they are central to the story—use passive voice and write, "The cookies were stolen." Alternatively, if you want to put the focus on the unknown thief, use active voice and write, "Somebody stole the cookies."

So remember, in a passive-voice sentence the subject of the sentence is the receiver of the action. Passive voice is not grammatically incorrect, and it is often a good choice when the actor isn't known or doesn't matter, or if you want to create some mystery around your sentence. On the other hand, it's often not the best choice. If you know who did what, it's often better to use an active voice.

OVERUSE OF *SO* AND *VERY*

A listener named Taryn asked if it is acceptable to write that she is "soooooo" happy that she is going to the prom, which got me thinking about not only the word *so* but also the word *very*.

Both words are often used as intensifiers, meaning they allow you to express that you are happier than just happy.

In the formal writing world, both words are looked down on, but *so* (by itself) is considered worse than *very*.

Misusing *So*

When you're speaking, emphasizing the word *so* seems to add punch to a simple statement—*I'm sooooo happy*—which is why Taryn is tempted to write the word with so many *o*'s: she's used to saying that she's "soooooo" happy, which is fine in informal conversation. But it should be avoided in writing.

On the other hand, when *so* is paired with *that,* it becomes more acceptable in writing.

> **Squiggly was *so* happy. (wrong)**
>
> **Squiggly was *so* happy *that* he jumped for joy. (right)**

When you say Squiggly was so happy that he jumped for joy, *so* becomes an adverb related to the degree of happiness instead of a vague intensifier. In other words, *so* leads into a thought about *how* happy Squiggly was. How happy was he? So happy *that he jumped for joy*.

Overusing Very

Unlike with the word *so,* it's not considered a mistake to use the word *very* by itself for emphasis. Nevertheless, you shouldn't overdo it. Instead of saying, "I was very hungry," it's typically better to search for a more creative adjective and write something like "I was famished" or "I was ravenous." Replacing two simple words like *very hungry* with one more descriptive word like *ravenous* makes your writing tighter and usually more interesting too.

Very as an intensifier also comes up when you're thinking of modifying absolutes (see page 66). Most grammar experts believe that *very* is out of place and not the best choice in phrases like *very unique* and *very dead* where it modifies something that doesn't have degrees.

Still, *very* shouldn't be banished from the language. *Merriam-Webster's Dictionary of English Usage* notes that E. B. White used the repetition of *very* to excellent effect in a letter, writing, "It was a day of very white clouds, very blue skies, and very dark green spruces." White is the coauthor of the famous style guide known as *Strunk and White* and formally titled *The Elements of Style,* and I agree that the repeated *very*s create a strong rhythm. The effect would be lost if White had written, "It was a day of snowy clouds, oceanic skies, and evergreen spruces."

In addition, *The Chicago Manual of Style* has numerous headings that include the word *very:* "Very Long Titles," "Very Wide Tables," "Very Large Numbers," and so on. It would seem silly if *Chicago*'s titles were something more creative like "Lengthy Titles," "Expansive Tables," and "Humongous Numbers." *Very long, very wide,* and *very large* get the point across more clearly (although *Chicago* could probably also get away with just *long, wide,* and *large*).

Finally, I shouldn't have to tell you this, but just to be safe, *very* is spelled v-e-r-y. *Vary* with an *a* (v-a-r-y) is a verb that means "to differ or change."

NIXING THE HORRID *OF:* PREPOSITIONS

Almost everyone has personal bad writing habits. One of mine is that I overuse the word *of.* I often go back through my documents looking for *of*s to delete. I'm not the only one; overusing *of* is a common writing problem.

Of is a preposition, and although not an inherently evil word, overusing it can make your writing sound passive and fussy. Here's an example of a bad sentence.

She is the wife of Sir Fragalot. (ick)

That's just horrible. It makes me cringe just to see it. The only time you should write something like that is to avoid a double possessive.

She is Sir Fragalot's wife.

(better)

She is the wife of Sir Fragalot's neighbor.

(acceptable to avoid a double possessive)

I'm hopeful that none of you would actually write, "She is the wife of Sir Fragalot," or any other such strained sentence. But that *of* can slip into your writing without being noticed if you aren't careful. Here's a more reasonable example: reporting on some bizarre science experiment, you might write the following: *The length of the string indicates how far the snail has moved.*

There's nothing really wrong with that sentence, except that it may leave you wondering how to attach a string to a snail. But you would probably explain that later in the paragraph.

Nevertheless, the sentence could be tightened up by rewriting it as the following: *The string length indicates how far the snail has moved.* See? *The length of the string* compared to *The string length*? It sounds more direct.

On the other hand, there are good ways to use the word *of*. For example, *Please bring me a bucket of water.* You have to write it that way to show that you want a bucket that actually has water in it. If you rewrote without the *of*—*Please bring me a water bucket*—you could be misinterpreted as asking for a bucket that is meant to hold water, but is currently empty.

Couple is also usually followed by *of,* as in *A couple of chickens crossed the road.*

Nevertheless, it's never a bad idea to search out your *of*s and make sure they are necessary.

AWKWARDNESS

Sometimes things aren't technically wrong or wordy; they're just painfully awkward.

When *The The* Isn't a Band

Imagine you're writing a lovely sentence, and then you run smack into a double *the*. Oh, the horror! You want to write "Have you heard the *The Fast and the Furious* sound track?" but you really don't want to write the second *the*. It's technically correct to write *the* twice, but whether it's right or wrong, if you turn that in to an English teacher, it will be circled with a red pen and marked "awk" for awkward. Rewrite the sentence to avoid the problem.

Sounds like?

A listener named Melanie sent me a story about mercury poisoning that talked about "fish-eating humans," and Melanie and I agreed that although the phrase is grammatically correct, we both initially thought the fish were eating people. Constructions such as *flesh-eating monster* or *man-eating lion* are so common that we are trained to initially think that a *something-eating anything* is attacking a person. Unless your intent is to be painfully clever, don't twist conventional phrases to mean the opposite of their standard use.

Foreign Words and Phrases

I generally don't like it when people use archaic or rare foreign words when an English word would do just as well. It's like standing on a chair and jeering "I know something you don't know!" It's a quick way to alienate the majority of your readers. On the other hand, I can see an argument for foreign phrases when they sum up something that is difficult to say in English. An example that comes to mind is the German word *schadenfreude* (which means to take joy in the misfortune of others). Still, spell out the meaning or resist the temptation to use foreign words if most of your readers will miss the point.

BLECHYUCKINESS: BUSINESS SPEAK

With regard to the meeting, are you tempted to utilize slides to facilitate understanding until everything is copasetic? Don't do it! Or people may be tempted to thump some sense into you with nearby whiteboard eraser.

It's called many things—business speak, officialese, bureaucratese—but I like listener Carol's name best: *blechyuckiness*. A major hallmark of blechyuckiness is substituting longer words for shorter, clearer words. What follows are examples, not a complete list.

Communicate Versus Tell

When you're tempted to use *communicate,* ask yourself if you really mean *tell. Communicate* has its place:

> **The couple had trouble communicating with each other.**
>
> **Having solar-powered transmitters improved the firemen's ability to communicate during emergencies.**

But there is no need to use *communicate* when you mean *tell.*

> **Please *communicate* to your team that we have a meeting on Friday. (ick)**
>
> **Please *tell* your team we have a meeting on Friday. (better)**

Use Versus Utilize

In most cases, *utilize* and *use* mean the same thing. *Utilize* has three syllables, *use* has one. When in doubt, use *use.*

Use and *utilize* are also potential signs of sloppy writing. When you see them, consider whether the sentence would be better without them.

Aardvark utilized the hammer to drive nails. (ick)

Aardvark used the hammer to drive nails. (acceptable)

Aardvark drove nails with the hammer. (better)

Facilitate Versus *Help, Plan, Hold,* Etc.

When you're tempted to write *facilitate*, ask yourself if you mean *help, plan, hold,* etc. Like *communicate, facilitate* has its place. It means "to make something easier":

Having the past presentations available will facilitate a more informed discussion.

Still, you could substitute "lead to" for "facilitate" in that sentence and it would sound less pretentious.

In the following sentences, *facilitate* is not the best choice.

~~Facilitate~~ Plan a meeting with your team.

Squiggly ~~facilitated~~ led the meeting.

Chapter 9
WORK IT

YOU NOW HAVE TOOLS THAT will help you be a clear, concise, and effective writer, and it may be time to take it to the next level, whatever that level may be. Maybe you want to work as a full-time staff writer, to work as a freelancer on the side, or to write and sell a short story or novel. Maybe you want to raise your profile at work and write an article for the company newsletter or website. Maybe you want to contribute to your school paper or church bulletin. If you're already a writer, maybe I have some tips you haven't thought of yet. Whatever your situation, here are some tips that should help you be a better working writer.

INTERVIEWING TIPS

If you want to write nonfiction, interviews will be a huge part of your job; and if you're interested in writing fiction, you may also conduct interviews to help develop your story, for example, to gather background or historical information. Conducting an interview is not the same as having a conversation.

Some of the best advice I got when I was starting out as a writer was to avoid the temptation to show the person you are interviewing how smart you are. And depending on your field, that can be really hard! I used to write magazine articles about science, so I was interviewing researchers who I thought were doing fascinating work. I have a master's degree in science, so it was hard to resist the temptation to show an amazing scientist that I knew my stuff and to avoid lapsing into jargon.

But if you fall into either of those traps, you're not going to get the quotes you need for your article or the full story that may help you think creatively about your novel. You need the people you are interviewing to explain what they know, in their own words. If you start showing off, you're going to put words in their mouth. Even worse, they'll realize you know the answers, and they won't tell you the important parts, leaving you to write about it without quotes.

A related issue is that it's important to avoid asking questions that will put the interviewee on the defensive. "Did you mutilate the cute snail after using it for your own purposes?" is not going to get you the same answer as, "What happens to the snails after the experiments are done?" Similarly, you don't want to ask leading questions. A leading question is a question that leads the person to the answer you want. For example, "Isn't that police inspector the nicest, cutest woman you've ever met?" After that kind of question, they're not likely to answer, "She's a horrid wench," which would actually be a great quote to get.

What this ends up meaning is that through most of the interview, you often sound like a dull, rather dense, but perhaps inquisitive lump of coal, interjecting questions such as "Can you tell me more about the police inspector?" or "Can you expand on the life cycle of the snail?"

Of course, this does not mean that you shouldn't do background research, or have interview questions prepared. You need to know where your story is going so you can probe in the right direction. You need to know the person's background and as much as you can about the topic of the interview. Although your job is mainly to get them talking and listen to what they say, you need to know when they say something of questionable accuracy, misspeak, get off track, or when there could be something interesting they forgot to mention. For example, it may be important to ask someone about an opposing theory they neglected to mention. For example, "OK, Dr. Jones, but what about the people who believe that your data is merely the result of tainted water?" It's helpful to understand the process behind their industry. For example, you may need to ask, "Well, Dr. Lopez—and I'm sure you have more insight on this than I do—how can you get your drug to market by fall 2008 when the typical trial takes four years?"

Now I'm going to share my secret weapon for interviewing with you. My last question is always, "Is there anything I haven't asked you that you think is important or worth talking about?" I ask that no matter how much preparing I do for an interview, and a third of the time that question got me something I hadn't anticipated.

STYLE GUIDES

It's true that when it comes to grammar there are a lot of hard-and-fast rules; but it's also true that there are hundreds, maybe thousands, of issues that are dictated by style. I know it would be so much easier if the rules were just black and white, and I could always just tell you what to do—I like to tell people what to do—but in a lot of cases you're going to have to decide on your own. You need a personal or corporate style guide.

Here's an example: I subscribe to an e-mail list for writers. There, the people are at each other's throats about how many spaces to put after a period at the end of a sentence—one or two. These people are surprisingly militant about spaces. Honestly, it kind of scares me; but regardless of what you think about the issue, the bottom line is that it's enough of an unresolved point that it's a matter of style. You should just find out what the style is of the people who have hired you, and do it that way. (See also the section on periods in chapter 4, "Punch Up Your Punctuation"; I'm a one-space girl myself.)

So, back to the point, this is where style guides come in. A style guide is a document that is typically put together by editors, managers, or producers to define how they want their writers to handle all the unresolved writing and grammar problems that arise (and, believe me, they do arise on an almost hourly basis). It can include almost anything the creator wants it to, but a style guide typically covers things like

- Punctuation
- Spelling
- Formatting
- General writing recommendations

A punctuation topic could be whether to capitalize the first letter of a full sentence after a colon. (I don't.) A spelling topic could be whether to use the American or British spelling of a word. (I use the American spelling.) A formatting topic could be what font to use for a specific section of the document or website. (If I'm referring to a specific word, I italicize it.) And finally, a general writing recommendation could be whether jargon is allowed. (I try not to use jargon.)

A style guide will keep editors from wasting time reworking documents to fit their preferences and from getting annoyed with writers for doing things "wrong."

A style guide will help companies and publications keep their work consistent, which makes their overall offering feel more professional. People may not consciously notice it, but they'll feel as if something is wrong if things aren't consistent from page to page. It is better to have one single style that some people don't agree with than to have different writers doing different things so that company documents are all willy-nilly. You don't want readers to end up thinking it's a disorganized, clueless company.

Writers in companies can also waste a lot of time trying to decide what to do (especially in organizations where people collaborate on documents). Trust me, I get a lot of e-mail messages that begin "My coworkers and I have been arguing about this for hours."

So, the quick and dirty tip is when you start a project with a new company or publication, always try to get the style guide; if you hire writers, make sure you have a style guide to give to them.

Keep in mind that different style guides have different uses. For example, *The Associated Press Stylebook* is primarily for writers who work at newspapers or news magazines; the *MLA Handbook for Writers of Research Papers* is obviously for writers of research papers, and it's used most commonly by people in the liberal arts and humanities. Writers of research papers in the sciences, on the other hand, may be more likely to use the *Publication Manual of the American Psychological Association* or *American Medical Association Manual of Style*. If I had to peg *The Chicago Manual of Style,* I'd say that its primary audience is book authors, but I love *Chicago* because it is one of the most comprehensive style guides, and I believe it's an essential backup for everyone.

GENERATING WRITING IDEAS

Working as a writer often means coming up with story ideas. The process is a bit different for fiction writing and nonfiction writing.

Generating Nonfiction Story Ideas

I made my living as a freelance magazine writer for a few years, so my ability to pay my bills rested on my ability to generate marketable story ideas. For the first couple of months it was difficult, but much to my surprise, after I wrote a few stories and became familiar with my target publications, I saw story ideas everywhere. Some days I would come up with as many as five story ideas. Some of them weren't great, but with that many to choose from, I could easily pick the winners.

For me, generating story ideas was all about having the right mindset and surrounding myself with people and publications. Here's some specific advice.

- **Adopt a curious mind-set.** You want to know the details about every-thing. I once got a great story idea for a science trade magazine from a friend's casual mention of a repetitive-stress injury. That initial brief comment led me to learn—and write—about lab workers who had to change careers because of repetitive pipetting injuries. If I hadn't been inquisitive, I wouldn't have learned that there was a story behind that initial brief comment.

- **Stay current.** When you know what's going on, you can spot trends and areas where different stories may intersect. Editors love trend sto-ries.

    When I was freelancing I subscribed to about twenty magazines and spent at least two hours each day reading news on the Internet. An example of a story that could come out of this type of undirected re-search is a piece about environmentally friendly weddings. A few years ago, green stories were popping up everywhere. I saw an unrelated article about weddings, and suddenly the idea of green weddings popped into my head.

- **Talk to people.** This may seem obvious, but most stories are about people. The more people you talk to, the better chance you have of stumbling upon a fantastic story. Also, when I was a science writer, al-most all my story ideas came from talking to scientists because they had better access to cutting-edge information than I did. I got new story ideas from scientists I was already interviewing and from scientists I met at conferences.

- **Identify target publications.** Keep a list of targeted publications in mind as you're out in the world. I've heard magazine editors complain about writers who pitch stories that aren't appropriate for the maga-zine. If you are intimately familiar with a publication and know what kinds of stories it runs, not only can you identify ideas, but you'll also write a pitch that's more likely to be accepted.

    For example, I knew I wanted to write for a trade publication called

The Scientist, so when I heard about a fire in a lab near my house, my mind was ready. I realized that *The Scientist* might be interested in a story about how to prepare a lab for an emergency if the story included a news hook about the fire. And, indeed, the publication snapped up the article.

In truth, stories are everywhere if your mind is prepared to look for them.

Generating Fiction Story Ideas

Now, on to fiction. For fiction stories, you need inspiration. And actually, getting inspiration for fiction writing isn't so different from searching for nonfiction story ideas.

It's still a good idea to read voraciously and interact with others. Fictional stories need characters, and you can get great inspiration from people you know or people you briefly encounter. When I was in college, I used to sit at coffee shops and people watch. I'd pick people who seemed interesting and make up stories about their lives.

Watching the public Twitter feed can also give you story ideas. You can watch until you see an intriguing post that inspires you, or you can challenge yourself by picking five random posts and forcing yourself to make a coherent story out of them. (And actually, if I were still a freelance magazine writer, I would also watch Twitter for nonfiction story ideas. It would be a great place to pick up on new trends.)

Another fun approach is to co-opt a minor character from another work to use as your starting point. The most famous example is probably the book *Wicked,* whose main character is the Wicked Witch of the West from *The Wizard of Oz,* but there are many examples. For instance, *Grendel* is a book about the monster in *Beowulf,* and *Rosencrantz & Guildenstern Are Dead* is a play, which was turned into a movie, about minor characters in Shakespeare's *Hamlet.* And, of course, fan fiction writers imagine new adventures for minor characters in their favorite TV shows, movies, and books.

A listener named Jurgen wrote in with a similar idea. He chooses two people from different news stories and imagines more about their lives and how they might interact with each other.

Keeping a journal can also be helpful. Flashes of inspiration can come at any time. It can help to have a journal where you write down ideas as they come and where you can keep track of your general reflections and your dreams as you are just waking up.

OVERCOMING WRITER'S BLOCK

Some days it just doesn't come together. You stare at the computer screen, but can't think of a thing to say. Or maybe you write, but you hate what you've written. Anything you do to overcome writer's block is just a mind game, but I don't mean that in a bad way because sometimes you have to play mind games to get your work done. Writing is a solitary experience; it's really all about you and your mind. Here are some things that work for me:

- **Don't play.** If you're going to procrastinate, force yourself to do something productive. Your choices are folding laundry or writing, not playing solitaire or writing. (Some people may advise you to take short, timed play breaks, but that doesn't work for me. If I start playing, it's harder to stop; and if I know I can do something fun instead of writing, I'll opt for the fun thing every time. Sometimes overcoming writer's block means forcing yourself to put in the time.)

- **Skip around.** Don't get too hung up on writing the first sentence or paragraph. If you have a great quote or plot point, and it falls in the middle of your story, write that first and come back to the beginning later. When I got stuck while writing this book, I'd jump to another section and work on that instead.

If you have multiple projects going at the same time, work on one of your other projects for a while. For example, I can always work on a

Grammar Girl podcast episode or edit a script for one of the other podcasts in the network.

- **Change location.** If I'm feeling bogged down, I take my laptop to the coffeehouse, library, or spare bedroom. A change of scenery can be inspiring and the act of packing and setting up my "office" somewhere else gives me that fresh-start feeling.

- **Try free writing.** When I was in college, I had a professor who forced us to do free-writing exercises. We had to sit at our desks and write without stopping for thirty minutes. It didn't matter what we wrote. She just watched to make sure that we were constantly putting pen to paper. The exercise was helpful, so you may want to give it a try if you are having a creative block. And a bonus is that it can also be a good way to come up with story ideas.

- **Get real deadlines.** Nothing focuses the mind like a deadline. So set yourself a deadline and try to make it as real as possible. If you don't have an editor setting deadlines for you, line up friends to read your story and tell them you'll deliver it at a certain time. Plan a date, but let yourself go out only if you finish your story. Maybe you're not like this, but I don't take a deadline seriously unless I know that something bad is going to happen if I don't finish on time. These days my podcast listeners are my "something bad" because I know they'll be unhappy if I release my show late.

  If you want to set real deadlines, meet other writers, and get feedback, one great way is to join (or start) a writing group. When I was freelance writing, I met with about eight writers every other week. We swapped stories for feedback, talked about our projects, and set goals for the next meeting. It was a wonderful experience, and many of those writers are still my good friends today. Taking a writing class at your local community college has a lot of the same benefits as joining a writing group and has the added benefit of giving you access to a formal instructor whose goal is to help you improve your writing.

Participating in writing contests can also help you set a deadline and get inspiration. I know of four contests with deadlines:

100-word Stories. *100-word Stories* is a blog and podcast that gives out a vague writing assignment every week and chooses a winner from the submissions.

Writers Weekly. The *Writers Weekly* website holds a quarterly short-story contest.

Writer's Digest. *Writer's Digest* has writing contests throughout the year and distributes weekly writing prompts.

NaNoWriMo. November is National Novel Writing Month and the NaNoWriMo.org website is where it all happens. Tens of thousands of people successfully write a fifty-thousand-word novel every year with the encouragement of other writers and the NaNoWriMo team.

PROOFREADING TIPS

I was surprised to discover that one of my most popular Grammar Girl podcasts is the episode with proofreading tips. I guess I'm not the only one to live through the horror of an embarrassing typo.

Here are a couple of big typo stories so you don't feel as if you're the only one.

- Someone at the Bank of Kazakh misspelled the word *bank* on the country's newly released notes in 2006, and the notes were printed and entered into circulation. How's that for a big, embarrassing proofreading problem?

- Also in 2006, Arizona had a typo on the election ballot, making the text on the ballot different from the text of the underlying law. (The proposition was for an $0.80-per-pack cigarette tax whereas the ballot read that people were voting for an "0.80 cent per pack cigarette tax," which equates to an $0.008-per-pack tax.) The proposition passed, and the interested parties went to court to determine which tax would apply. What an expensive and unfortunate typo!

Over time I have come to believe that it's nearly impossible for people to accurately proofread their own writing. Typos are bad and can get you in a lot of trouble; but even though you should do your best to catch them, I also think it's important not to beat yourself up too badly when typos happen. Human error is inevitable. The real key to avoiding typos is to have someone else proofread your copy. Which brings me to something people always ask me: why is writing on the Internet so bad?

Bloggers Don't Have Copy Editors

In addition to the fact that most people don't get a good grammar education, I believe a significant reason you see so many typos and errors on websites is that most Web copy goes live without ever being reviewed by anyone but the writer. By contrast, copy you see in newspapers and magazines (in addition to being written by professional writers) goes through an extensive editing process. After a writer turns in a story, it's usually reviewed by multiple editors, including the department editor who assigned it, a senior editor, and a copy editor. Of course these editors all have more training in grammar and writing than the average person writing a blog. Commercial websites, in my experience, fall somewhere between magazines and blogs—these companies tend to run lean editorial departments and may have only one editor looking at copy before it goes live. (For example, at the Quick and Dirty Tips website, only one copy editor reviews our articles before they go live.)

Who's Your Daddy, er, Proofreader?

The best advice I can give you for avoiding typos is to have someone else proofread your work. On the other hand, I know this isn't possible for things like e-mail messages or rushed projects, so here are eight more proofreading tips I've collected over the years.

1. Read your work backward, starting with the last sentence and working your way in reverse order to the beginning. Supposedly, this works better than reading through from the beginning because your brain knows what you meant to write, so you tend to skip over errors when you're reading forward.

2. Read your work out loud. This forces you to read each word individually and increases the odds that you'll find a typo. This works quite well for me, and most of the typos that make it into my transcripts seem to be things you wouldn't catch by reading aloud, such as misplaced commas. A listener who works in a crowded office shared a funny secret with me: he pretends to be talking on the phone while he reads his work aloud to himself so his coworkers don't think he's crazy.

3. Make your computer read to you. Most computers these days come with software, designed for the visually impaired, that will read the text to you. You can put on your headphones and listen to the robotic computer voice read your masterpiece. It won't catch problems with words that sound alike (e.g., *it's* versus *its*) but you'll definitely hear missing or mangled words. (Search for "text to speech" in the Help section of your word-processing software.)

4. Force yourself to view each word. If you don't want to read out loud, you can force yourself to consider each word by using the tip of a pencil or pen to physically touch each word. You can also force yourself to focus on smaller sections of the document by putting a ruler under each line of text as you are reading or by cutting out a small rectangular window on an index card and sliding it over your copy as you read.

5. Always proofread a printed version of your work. I don't know why, but if I try to proofread on a computer monitor, I always miss more errors than if I print out a copy of my work and go over it on paper.

6. Use the auto-correct feature. I also call this the "know thyself" trick. For example, I always type *pateint* instead of *patient*. Always. But with the auto-correct feature in my word-processing software, I can tell the computer that every time I typed *pateint* it should insert *patient*. Problem solved!

7. Give yourself some time. If possible, let your work sit for a while before you proofread it. I'm just speculating here, but it seems to me that if you are able to clear your mind and approach the writing from a fresh perspective, then your brain is more able to focus on the actual words, rather than seeing the words you think you wrote.

8. Use a spell checker. Don't forget to run your work through your computer's spell-checking tool. It won't find every error, and you shouldn't rely exclusively on spell check, but you should be doubly embarrassed if you turn in something or publish it with an error that spell check would have caught.

THE END OF THE BOOK, BUT THE BEGINNING FOR YOU

If you made it this far, I hope I've given you the tools you need to write with confidence. I think of grammar and usage as the rules to the game of writing, and the rules are just the building blocks of creativity. Writing proper sentences doesn't ensure that your work will be brilliant and inspiring, but knowing the rules can keep errors from marring your brilliance and inspiration.

Never let fear of making mistakes keep you from writing. Just do your best. If you find that you are too intimidated while writing, forget about the rules in your first draft and go back over the piece later with a specific eye for grammar and usage rules. Look things up if you don't know them. If something wasn't covered in this book, you can likely find it in a dictionary, usage guide, or style guide. If someone marks up your writing with a big red pen, consider it a learning experience and go on.

At a minimum, take your newfound skills and write a kind and witty e-mail message to a friend to brighten their day. Write your grandmother a letter that will make her proud. Make this year's holiday newsletter shine.

If you've never written something public before, why not give it a try? Do you live in a small town and love to read? Ask the local newspaper if you can occasionally review books for their paper. Start a blog about something you love or a topic related to your job. Revise that forgotten short story one more time, and send it out to literary magazines—who knows what may happen?

If you're already a working writer, well, you already know what to do. Just keep this book and your other favorites handy for times when you forget where you should put a comma or when to use *whom*. Make your copy editor's job a little easier.

Now, go forth and write!

GRAMMAR PARTY AT MY PLACE!

IF YOU HAVE MORE QUESTIONS you can subscribe to the free weekly Grammar Girl podcast at iTunes, at the Zune Marketplace, or at the Quick and Dirty Tips website (www.quickanddirtytips .com) where you can also subscribe to the free e-mail newsletter I send out every week (or so) with a free grammar tip. You can also write (feed back@quickanddirtytips.com) or call in and leave a recorded question (206-338-4475)—you may hear it answered on the show!

Appendices

SENTENCE ADVERBS

Sentence adverbs are words that modify a whole sentence. Examples of sentence adverbs include the following:

Clearly

Fortunately

Frankly

Happily

Honestly

Hopefully*

Ironically

Mercifully

Remarkably

Thankfully

Unfortunately

---

*Using *hopefully* as a sentence adverb is controversial.

CONJUNCTIVE ADVERBS

Conjuctive adverbs are transitional words that join two clauses that could be independent sentences. Use a semicolon before the conjunctive adverb to join two clauses. (See page 73 for a discussion of using *however* as a conjuctive adverb.) Examples of words that can be used as conjunctive adverbs include the following: .

Accordingly

Again

Also

Anyway

Besides

Certainly

Consequently

Finally

Furthermore

Hence

However

Incidentally

Indeed

Instead

Likewise

Meanwhile

Moreover

Namely

Nevertheless

Next

Nonetheless

Otherwise

Similarly

Specifically

Still

Subsequently

Then

Therefore

Thus

SUBORDINATING CONJUNCTIONS

Subordinating conjunctions join subordinate clauses to other clauses.
See page 77 for a discussion of *because* as a subordinating conjunction.
Following is a list of common subordinating conjunctions:

After

Although

As

As if

As in

As long as

Because

Before

Despite

Even though

How

If

Lest
Now that
Once
Provided
Rather than
So that
Since
Than
That
Though
Unless
Until
When
Whenever
Where
Whereas
Whether
While

LINKING VERBS

A linking verb can also be called a copula.

Verbs That Are Always Linking Verbs

Be (is, was, are, were, have been, had been, am being, etc.)
Become
Seem

Verbs That Are Sometimes Linking Verbs and Sometimes Action Verbs

This list contains the most common words that can function as linking verbs or action verbs. Note how it is possible to replace the verb with a form of *to be* in each sentence without dramatically changing the meaning. (See pages 15, 31, and 144 for more discussion of linking verbs.)

Verb	Example as a Linking Verb
Appear	It appears hot.
Feel	I feel energetic.
Get	He got himself fired.
Grow	We grow weary.
Lie	The fields lie fallow.
Look	She looks happy.
Prove	It proved futile.
Remain	He remains angry.
Smell	It smells fragrant.
Sound	The music sounds loud.
Stay	They will stay together.
Taste	It tastes salty.
Turn	Her face turned red.

COMMON IRREGULAR VERBS

Regular verbs take their past-tense form by adding *-d* or *-ed*. Irregular verbs don't follow these typical conjugation rules. Here are some of the common irregular verbs.

Present Tense	Past Tense	Present Tense	Past Tense
arise	arose	bear	bore
awake	awoke	beat	beat
be	was, were, been	become	became

Present Tense	Past Tense	Present Tense	Past Tense
begin	began	fight	fought
bend	bent	find	found
bet	bet	fit	fit
bind	bound	flee	fled
bite	bit	fling	flung
bleed	bled	fly	flew
blow	blew	forbid	forbade
break	broke	foresee	foresaw
breed	bred	forget	forgot
bring	brought	forgive	forgave
build	built	forsake	forsook
burst	burst	freeze	froze
bust	bust	get	got
buy	bought	give	gave
cast	cast	go	went
catch	caught	grind	ground
choose	chose	grow	grew
cling	clung	handwrite	handwrote
come	came	hang	hung
cost	cost	have	had
creep	crept	hide	hid
cut	cut	hit	hit
deal	dealt	hold	held
dig	dug	hurt	hurt
do	did	inlay	inlaid
draw	drew	keep	kept
drive	drove	knit	knit
drink	drank	know	knew
dwell	dwelt	lay	laid
eat	ate	lead	led
fall	fell	leave	left
feed	fed	lend	lent
feel	felt	let	let

Present Tense	Past Tense	Present Tense	Past Tense
lie	lay	shoot	shot
lose	lost	shrink	shrank
make	made	shut	shut
mean	meant	sing	sang
meet	met	sink	sank
mislead	misled	sit	sat
mistake	mistook	slay	slew
overcome	overcame	sleep	slept
overdraw	overdrew	slide	slid
overdo	overdid	sling	slung
overtake	overtook	slit	slit
overthrow	overthrew	smite	smote
pay	paid	speak	spoke
put	put	speed	sped
quit	quit	spend	spent
read	read (same	spin	spun
	spelling,	split	split
	different	spread	spread
	pronunciation)	stand	stood
rid	rid	steal	stole
ride	rode	stick	stuck
ring	rang	sting	stung
rise	rose	stink	stank
run	ran	stride	strode
say	said	strike	struck
see	saw	string	strung
seek	sought	strive	strove
sell	sold	swear	swore
send	sent	sweep	swept
set	set	swim	swam
shake	shook	swing	swung
shed	shed	take	took
shine	shone	teach	taught

Present Tense	Past Tense	Present Tense	Past Tense
tear	tore	wear	wore
tell	told	wed	wed
think	thought	weep	wept
throw	threw	wind	wound
thrust	thrust	win	won
tread	trod	withdraw	withdrew
understand	understood	withhold	withheld
uphold	upheld	withstand	withstood
upset	upset	wring	wrung
wake	woke	write	wrote

Grammar Girl's Strunk & Twite: A Twitter Style Guide (in which every entry is < 141 characters)

Don't start posts with *I am*. You are answering the question, "What are you doing? It's OK to answer with fragments in a conversation.

Use proper capitalization. Typing in lowercase doesn't save characters; it's just lazy.

Use proper basic punctuation. It helps people understand what you mean.

Don't use abbreviations such as 4u and l8 and brb. They make you sound like a twelve-year-old (which is bad, unless you actually are a twelve-year-old).

Use contractions whenever possible.

Shorthand symbols such as >, =, &, and @ are allowed.

Shortened word forms such as *nite* and *thru* are allowed.

Use numerals, not words, for all numbers.

Provide links and context whenever possible. Remember that many of your followers can't see what you are responding to.

Use tinyurl.com or urltea.com to shorten links.

If you can't say it in 140 characters, reevaluate whether you should be posting it at Twitter.

Bibliography

THE FIVE BOOKS I'D RATHER NOT LIVE WITHOUT

Brians, P. *Common Errors in English Usage.* Wilsonville, Ore.: William, James & Co., 2003.

The Chicago Manual of Style. 15th ed. Chicago: University of Chicago Press, 2003.

Garner, B. *Garner's Modern American Usage.* Oxford: Oxford University Press, 2003.

Goldstein, N., ed. *The Associated Press Stylebook and Libel Manual.* Reading, Penn.: Perseus Books, 1998.

Shaw, H. *Punctuate It Right!* New York: Harper Paperbacks, 1993.

OTHER RESOURCES I USED TO WRITE THIS BOOK

The American Heritage Guide to Contemporary Usage and Style. Boston: Houghton Mifflin Company, 2005.

Burchfield, R. W., ed. *The New Fowler's Modern English Usage.* 3rd ed. New York: Oxford University Press, 1996.

Casagrande, J. *Grammar Snobs Are Great Big Meanies.* New York: Penguin Books, 2006.

Dictionary.com. *Dictionary.com Unabridged (v 1.1).* Random House, Inc., http://dictionary.reference.com.

Lutz, G., and D. Stevenson. *The Writer's Digest Grammar Desk Reference.* Cincinnati: Writer's Digest Books, 2005.

Lynch, J. *Lynch Guide to Grammar,* http://andromeda.rutgers.edu/ ~jlynch/Writing.

McArthur, T., ed. *Oxford Companion to the English Language.* Oxford: Oxford University Press, 2002.

Merriam-Webster's Dictionary of English Usage. Springfield, Mass.: Merriam-Webster, 1994.

O'Connor, P. *Woe Is I.* New York: Penguin Putnam, 1996.

Straus, J. *The Blue Book of Grammar and Punctuation.* 9th ed. Mill Valley, Calif.: Jane Straus, 2006.

Strumpf, M., and A. Douglas. *The Grammar Bible.* New York: Henry Holt and Company, 2004.

Walsh, B. *Lapsing Into a Comma.* Chicago: Contemporary Books, 2004.

Quick and Dirty Grammar at a Glance

I bet you thought grammar couldn't get any more quick and dirty than it did in the previous pages, but here's the quickest grammar of all, culled from lengthier explanations found elsewhere in this book. Sometimes you just need a quick fix.

A/An: Use *a* before consonant sounds; use *an* before vowel sounds. *She has an MBA. It's a Utopian idea.*

A Lot: *A lot* means "a large number" and is two words, not one. *Allot* means "to parcel out."

Abbreviations (Making Them Plural): Add an *s* (without an apostrophe) to the end of an abbreviation to make it plural. *Smith had two RBIs tonight.*

Affect/Effect: Most of the time *affect* is a verb and *effect* is a noun. *He affected her. The effect mattered.* (Exceptions, p. 11.)

Assure/Ensure/Insure: *Assure* means "to reassure"; *ensure* means "to guarantee"; *insure* refers to insurance.

Because: It's OK to start a sentence with *because;* just be sure you haven't created a sentence fragment. *Because Squiggly was tired, he forgot to stow the chocolate.* (OK) *Because Squiggly was tired.* (wrong)

Between You and I/Between You and Me: *Between you and me* is the correct phrase.

Can/May: Traditionalists maintain that *can* refers to ability and *may* refers to permission. *Can you fix the broken dishwasher? May I go to the mall?*

Capital/Capitol: *Capital* refers to a city, uppercase letter, or wealth. A *capitol* is a building.

Colons: In sentences, only use colons after something that would be a complete sentence on its own.

Commas (Equal Pauses): It is *not* a rule that you put a comma in wherever you would naturally pause in a sentence.

Comma (Serial): It's up to you whether to use a serial comma (the comma before the final *and* in a list of items).

Complement/Compliment: Things that work well together complement each other. Compliments are a form of praise.

Dead: *Dead* is an absolute (nongradable) word that shouldn't be modified with words such as *completely* or *very*.

Different From/Different Than: In most cases, *different from* is the preferred form.

E.G./I.E.: *E.g.* means "for example"; *i.e.* means "that is."

Each/Every: *Each* and *every* are singular and mean the same thing.

E-mail/Email: Both forms are acceptable. Traditionalists prefer *e-mail*.

Everyone/Everybody: *Everyone* and *everybody* are singular and mean the same thing.

Farther/Further: *Farther* refers to physical distance; *further* relates to metaphorical distance or means "moreover." *Aardvark ran farther than Squiggly. Further, they hope to run tomorrow.*

Fewer/Less: Use *fewer* for count nouns; use *less* for mass nouns. *There were fewer fish. There was less water.*

Hanged/Hung: People (or animals) who were executed were hanged; everything else was hung.

Hopefully: Although it isn't wrong, don't start a sentence with *hopefully*—too many people believe it's wrong.

However: It's OK to start a sentence with *however,* but be careful with your comma placement. *However, we wish he hadn't used permanent ink. However hard Squiggly tried, he couldn't reach the chocolate.*

Hyphen: Never use a hyphen in place of a dash.

In To/Into: *Into* is a preposition that specifies a direction; sometimes the words *in* and *to* just end up next to each other. *Move into the foyer. He broke in to the dining room.*

Internet: *Internet* is capitalized.

Its/It's: *Its* is the possessive form of *it; it's* means "it is" or "it has." *It's a shame the tree lost its leaves.*

Lay/Lie: Subjects lie down; objects are laid down. *I want to lie down. I will lay the pen on the table.*

Literally: *Literally* means "exactly." Don't use it for emphasis or to mean "figuratively."

Log In/Log On/Log Out/Log Off: These are all acceptable two-word verbs. They require a hyphen when used as adjective. *I want to log in. Please give me the log-in code.*

May/Might: *May* implies more of a likelihood that something is possible than *might. We may go out. Pigs might fly.*

Modifiers (Misplaced): Make sure your modifiers apply to the right words. *I only eat chocolate.* (The only thing I do with chocolate is eat it.) *I eat only chocolate.* (I eat nothing but chocolate.)

Myself: Please visit Aardvark and myself is an incorrect hypercorrection. The correct form is *Please visit Aardvark and me.*

Nauseated/Nauseous: *Nauseated* means you feel queasy; *nauseous* describes something that makes you queasy. *The nauseous fumes are making me nauseated.*

Nouns (Collective): Collective nouns describe a group of things such as furniture and a team. They are singular in the United States.

Numbers (at the Beginning of a Sentence): Write out numbers at the beginning of a sentence.

Online/On Line: *Online* is one word, not two.

Periods (Abbreviations at the End of a Sentence): Don't use two periods if you have an abbreviation at the end of a sentence.

Periods (Spaces After): Use one space after a period at the end of a sentence.

Possession (Compound): When two people share something, they share an apostrophe. When two people have separate things, they each need their own apostrophe. *We're at Squiggly and Aardvark's house. Have you met Squiggly's and Aardvark's mothers?*

Possession (Words That End with *S*): The most common way to make a singular word that ends with *s* possessive is to add a lone apostrophe (*Steve Jobs' keynote*), but it's not wrong to add an *s* after the apostrophe (*Steve Jobs's keynote*). Some people make the decision based on pronunciation (*Steve Jobs' keynote, Kansas's statute*).

Prepositions (Ending Sentences with): It's OK to end a sentence with a preposition, except when the preposition is dispensable. *Whom did you step on?* (OK) *Where is he at?* (wrong)

Question Marks (with Indirect Questions): Don't use a question mark after an indirect question. *I wonder why Squiggly left.*

Question Marks (with Question Tags): Use question marks after statements that end with question tags. *Squiggly left because he was mad, didn't he?*

Quote/Quotation: *Quote* is a verb; *quotation* is a noun. *I want to quote you. Is this the correct quotation?*

Quotation Marks (with Other Punctuation): Commas and periods go inside of quotation marks; colons and semicolons go outside of quotation marks. Question marks and exclamation points can go inside or outside of quotation marks, depending on the context.

Sentences (Run-on): Run-on sentences aren't just long sentences; they are created when main clauses are joined without proper punctuation.

Sic: *Sic* is Latin for "thus so." You can use [sic] to show that an error occurred in the original text—you know there's an error and you didn't introduce it.

Sit/Set: Subjects sit, objects are set. *I want to sit down. I will set the pen on the table.*

Split Infinitives: It's OK to split infinitives. *They want to boldly go where no one has gone before.*

Subject/Object: The subject in a sentence takes the action; the object receives or is the target of the action. *[Subject] threw the ball. Squiggly threw the [object].*

Than/Then: Use *than* for comparison; use *then* for time. *Aardvark is taller than Squiggly. Then they went fishing.*

That/Which: Use *that* with restrictive clauses; use *which* with nonrestrictive clauses. *I like gems that sparkle, including diamonds, which are expensive.*

That/Who: Use *that* to refer to things; use *who* to refer to people.

The: Pronounce as "thuh" before consonant sounds, "thee" before vowel sounds.

Unique: *Unique* is an absolute (nongradable) word that shouldn't be modified with words such as *most* or *very.*

Verbs (Action and Linking): Use adverbs to modify action verbs and adjectives to modify linking verbs. *He ran terribly. He smells terrible.*

Was/Were: Use *was* to refer to the past; use *were* to refer to things that are wishful or not true. *I was at the store. If I were rich, I would buy a yacht.*

Who/Whom: Use *who* to refer to a subject; use *whom* to refer to an object. *Who loves Squiggly? Whom do you love?*

Your/You're: *Your* is the possessive form of you; *you're* means "you are."

Acknowledgments

I'd like to thank The Kind Grind in Santa Cruz, California, where the idea for the Grammar Girl podcast hit me and where I did some of the early work on the manuscript, and Java Jungle in Reno, Nevada, where much of this book was written. Both coffeehouses have local art, eclectic music, and all-around wonderfully inspiring environments.

It may seem strange, but I'd like to thank Apple and the iTunes team for making it easy to buy and listen to the music that accompanied me as I wrote this book, and for providing the first platform that made it easy to freely distribute my podcast—without the podcast there would be no book. And, of course, there would also be no podcast (and therefore no book) without the podcast listeners who download the show every week and who send me encouraging notes, funny photos, interesting questions, and criticism when I need it. It's much more fun with you around.

My parents also deserve recognition. Steve and Amy Bess, in addition to being generally supportive, helped during the crunch time when I needed to finish writing this book and finish remodeling my house at the same time. (Don't worry, they helped with the remodeling, not the writing.) Gail and Dave Phelps provide faithful support even though they aren't as near, and they love me even when I misplace a modifier or fall flat on my face. The late Guy and Janette Coughlin gave me a safe and happy childhood and put so much emphasis on my education over everything else that to this day I am unable to complete many household tasks that are second nature to a typical adult. (But I *am* Grammar Girl, so I believe they would be proud.)

Many people at Henry Holt and Company also made this book possible and helped along the way. Publisher John Sterling saw my vision for the entire Quick and Dirty Tips enterprise, including Grammar Girl, and protected my time when I needed to sit down and just write for a couple of months. In that vein, I'd also like to thank Richard Rhorer, the Quick and Dirty Tips executive producer, who time and again kept the rest of the business moving forward while I was writing this book. And, of course, Helen Atsma, my editor at Henry Holt and Company, who kept me on schedule and provided excellent advice.

Other people also worked behind the scenes to keep the business, podcast, and book on track. Although any errors remain my own, freelance copy editors Steve Thornton and Bonnie Trenga take turns copyediting the Grammar Girl podcast every week, and Muriel Jorgensen copyedited this book. It takes a special kind of person to edit someone called Grammar Girl, and I always enjoy our back-and-forth discussions about style issues. In addition, my assistant, Cherylyn Feierabend (also known as the Mighty Mommy), has proven time and again that my trust in her is well placed.

Last but not least, I'd like to thank my husband, Pat, for his unflagging support and uncanny ability to make me laugh. I could have written the book without him, but it wouldn't have been as fun.

Index

About the Author

MIGNON FOGARTY is the creator of Grammar Girl and founder of the Quick and Dirty Tips Network. A technical writer and entrepreneur, she has served as an editor and producer at a number of health and science websites. She has a B.A. in English from the University of Washington in Seattle and an M.S. in biology from Stanford University. She lives in Reno, Nevada, with her husband, Patrick. Visit her website at http://grammar.quickanddirtytips.com/.